WHEN WE WERE
BOUNCERS

GW00675443

Paul 'The Mauler' Lazenby

PUNCH INNA FACE PUBLICATIONS
A division of 667765 BC Ltd.

Vancouver, Canada

PUNCH INNA FACE PUBLICATIONS
A division of 667765 BC Ltd.

208–179 Davie St.

Vancouver, BC, Canada V6Z 2Y1

Covers by Dacosta! at Chocolate Soop

ISBN 978-0-9938218-1-3

Available from Amazon.com, CreateSpace.com, and other retail outlets.

DISCLAIMER

Certain names, places, and other details
have been changed to protect the guilty.

Other names, places and details were left
unchanged because the guilty don't give a fuck.

This book is dedicated to
every bouncer who ever had my back
when it mattered.

In Memory of

DARREN SHAHLAVI
MIKE NYHUIS
ALEX GREEN
SHAWN ROBINSON

and

TONY MORELLI

TABLE OF CONTENTS

INTRODUCTION

Before They Were Famous,
They Were Bouncers.

That's the idea that hit me at the end of a shift one night, as I lounged around trading war stories with a bunch of fellow doormen. As tales of brutal violence, gut-busting hilarity and lascivious back-room debauchery flew fast and furious, it occurred to me that there must be a ton of famous and accomplished people who've also put in time behind the velvet rope, and have their own unbelievable stories.

Then I realized that, having been lucky enough to rub shoulders and trade blows with many of them in my fighting, wrestling and film/TV careers, I was in the unique position of being able to collect those stories and share them with the world.

What I didn't realize though, was how ill-prepared I'd be for the downright insanity of those on-and-off-duty tales of mayhem. Even with over twenty years of security experience under my belt, I simply did not see a lot of this shit coming. And deciding to draw from similar professions like bodyguard and security guard yielded even more crazy goodness, to the point that I was quickly buried neck-deep in a giant, steaming pile of awesome.

If you have half as much fun reading this stuff as I had compiling it, you're gonna lose your damn mind before you're halfway through. And if you don't, then there has gotta be something wrong with you because this shit is seriously MAD BOSS COOL.

Paul "The Mauler" Lazenby
Vancouver, BC, Canada
April 2015
🐦 *@FamousBouncers*

Chapter One

RENZO GRACIE

All photos courtesy Susumu Nagao.

"I keep choking him out and I whisper, 'This is what death feels like!'"

A cousin of UFC Hall-of-Famer Royce Gracie, Renzo has spent the past twenty-plus years carving out his own legend in the MMA and grappling worlds. Renzo's career accolades include a World Combat Championship tournament title, a Martial Arts Reality Superfight title, and back-to-back ADCC world submission grappling championships.

But as respected as he is as a fighter, Renzo is even more respected as a person, being one of the friendliest, most humble and gregarious individuals whom I have ever crossed paths with. Even people who, for whatever reason, have less-than-complimentary things to say about the Gracie family will nearly always go out of their way to add: "Except Renzo."

Currently, Renzo operates the wildly-successful chain of Renzo Gracie Jiu-jitsu Academies, overseeing the training of a laundry list of MMA and jiu-jitsu warriors.

Rumble in the Jungle

When I was fourteen years old, I was a bouncer in a whorehouse in the Amazon.

This was in the city of Manaus, in Brazil, where me and a very good friend of mine were living. I was fourteen and he was sixteen, and we raised some money to go to the "ladies' house." But when we get there and we sit down to wait for a room to be vacant, a huge problem arise.

A guy, he didn't wanna pay and it was a mess. He started pushing the ladies around and so the bouncer came in, an older guy. And when the bouncer came in, the guy head butt him and knock him out! I just think, "Oh, man, this is it! I was able to put the money together to come here and enjoy a good time, and now this guy's gonna ruin everything!"

So I look at my friend and I say, "You shoot on the legs, I am gonna choke him out." So my friend [dove forward and grabbed] his legs, and I jump on his back and choke him out! And after I choke him, I grab his wallet and pay the lady what he owe, and then I wake him up and kick him out, tell him not to come back.

Renzo dropping bombs on Shungo Oyama in Japan's Pride Fighting Championships.

When the bouncer woke up, he saw what happened and right away he ask us to work there with him. So we did work there, helping him. In reality, it was a great thing because before that, I didn't have [anything] to eat, anywhere to sleep, and they hook me up with everything. I stay there for three months and a half, and I not only work as a bouncer in a nice house, but they even give me the ladies' service for free! It was unbelievable! (laughs)

Hollywood Rock

A few years later I was working at a huge concert in Rio called "Hollywood Rock." I was taking care of the sound tower, and as I'm sitting up there I heard a huge discussion down [below me]. I look down, and I recognize the guy who the bouncers are having a problem with, so I go down there to solve the problem.

As I get there, I see they don't wanna let the guy come in. The guy keeps telling them, "I have to come in to fix the sound! I'm gonna play next and I have to fix this!" And the bouncer goes, "You don't have the credentials, you can't walk in! I don't care who you are!" But the guy is pleading with him, "I have to come in, I'm playing next, I have to do this!"

So I come over and I say, "Guys, we have to let him in," and the bouncer goes, "Renzo, you're too nice with everybody all the time! We can not! The orders is not to let those who don't have credentials in!"

And then I say, "Guys! BON JOVI has to come in to fix the sound!" It was Jon Bon Jovi, the singer of one of my favorite bands! (laughs) So I grab Bon Jovi, I bring him in, and he took care of [the sound] and they played an unbelievable show.

On the same concert, we had a guy at one of the entrances who was insulting everybody and spitting at the bouncers, but because the press was there to witness everything, nobody could do anything about the guy. So the head of security call me on the radio and say, "We have a problem at Gate Six." At the time, I was working at Gate Four, so I leave my gate without my shirt, without credentials, without nothing. I [arrive at] Gate Six running, and right away I get into a fight with this guy and I beat him up. Then I run back to Gate Four and put my shirt and credentials back on! (laughs)

Whenever I work in that place, that was my job—if a problem had no solution, I would come [wearing no identification] to beat them up and leave, and even the other security guys didn't know what happened! Only the head of security knows, because he was a very good friend of mine and I was always giving him a hand. (laughs) Some unbelievable moments I had!

A 140-Character Mugging

Mauler's Note: This next story has nothing to do with bouncing, but there was NO WAY I was gonna get Renzo on the phone and not ask him to recreate the night he became the first man in history to live-tweet his own attempted mugging.

Not long ago in New York, I was leaving a restaurant late at night, and I went to an ATM machine. There was two guys there arguing about getting money or not, and so I say, "Fuck it, I'm gonna walk." But when I took off walking they start following me, you know? They probably thought I was drunk because I was on Twitter on my phone and I was weaving, you know, from one side [of the sidewalk] to the other. When I notice that they follow me, I know what is probably coming so I start describing it on Twitter, letting the people know what is happening. How much of a rush it was, just like at home in Brazil! (laughs)

In New York, the criminals like to rob people who work at the restaurants because normally they have cash with them, from tips, you know? So maybe those guys thought I work in the restaurant I came out of, because they came after me [saying] "Gimme a cigarette, gimme a cigarette!" The criminals are doing this a lot now—when they want to get close to you, they say "gimme a dollar" or they ask for a cigarette.

So I look at them and say, "I don't smoke," but they keep coming. They run and grab me by the arm and reach inside my pocket, "Gimme a cigarette!" I was looking to see a gun [on them] or at least a knife, you know? But then I see they are [unarmed and] just trying to use muscle to get my wallet. And so I think, "Bad mistake for you guys!" (laughs)

I knock the first one out with a left hook and a straight [right] hand and he fell. But when I went to grab the second guy, he was able to take off. I grab his shirt but he [pulled free and] ran. So as the first one was waking up, I put a beating on him and then I take a picture of him for Twitter! (laughs) And then I go back to my car to go after the second one, driving.

I sit in my car, and I watch the first one when he gets up and walks away. I see the direction that he goes, and then I drive [in that direction] with the car. [At first] I can't see the second guy, and I'm about to go home but then I find him waiting for his friend on Eleventh Avenue! So I park, and I go back and get that second guy in a corner.

First I choke him out, and then I use my fist to give him some nice "raccoon eyes," you know? (laughs) Then I keep choking him out, several times. I choke him out, I let him wake up, I whisper in his ear "This is what death feels like!" and then I choke him out again! (laughs) I think I scare them a little—for sure we now have two new-born Christians roaming the streets of New York! (laughs)

Only a few weeks after this happens, a guy approaches me on the street and asks me for a lighter, "Where's your lighter?" I start laughing because I thought he was cracking a joke about the story with the two guys, but in reality he was not. It was a guy trying to hustle some money out of me, you know? When I realize this, I start walking toward him and say, "I didn't bring no lighter, because if I had one, I would set your ass on fire!"

And he goes, "I need no lighter!" and runs away! (laughs)

 *@RenzoGracieBJJ*

 *www.RenzoGracie.com*

Chapter Two

ADAM 'EDGE' COPELAND

Photo courtesy Joyce Paustian.

> *"I didn't realize those guys were gonna get their shit right in the girls' faces and just SHAKE it. I don't know if that was legal or not, but it was sure goin' on."*

Boy, has this guy ever come a long way from his days of wrestling with the likes of me in a 10x10 foot ring in northern Manitoba.

From humble beginnings in his native Orangeville, Ontario, Canada, Adam "Edge" Copeland built a 20-year wrestling career that includes more total title reigns than any performer in World Wrestling Entertainment history (including a tag team title reign with his childhood hero, Hulk Hogan). But after cementing his status as one of the greatest WWE superstars ever, Adam found himself forced into early retirement by serious neck injuries. As a testament to the impact that Adam had on the business to which he devoted his life, he became the youngest-ever inductee into the WWE Hall of Fame only months after hanging up his boots.

At the time of this writing, Adam is focusing on his acting career, which includes a recurring role as Police Chief Dwight Hedrickson on the TV series *Haven*.

But before all that, he was just a skinny, dorky teenager trying not to get his ass handed to him in a small-town Ontario nightclub.

O'Toole's

I started bouncing at seventeen years old in my hometown of Orangeville, at a franchise place called O'Toole's. Of course it was highly illegal for me to be doing that, but even at that age, I was about six foot four and two hundred twenty, and they were short on bouncers.

One thing about Orangeville was that, even though it was a small town of about 15,000 people, it was surrounded by a bunch of farming communities whose farm boys would come into town with their shit-kickers on when they wanted to drink. And when the drinking started, all the different rivalries from all the different towns would flare up.

The bouncing crew included friends of mine named Doug Childs and Kelly McGoogan, as well as the legendary "Burt the Hurt." Burt was a guy I knew from the wrestling business, we were both training to be wrestlers at Sully's Gym in Toronto. In his day job, he was a schoolteacher, but he was also legally blind, so how he got a license,

I have no idea. Burt was also INSANE—he would only answer if you called him by his full name of "Burt the Hurt," and he spoke about himself in the third person way before The Rock ever did. I liked to call him "The Innovator of Eccentricity" because he always talked as if he was cutting a wrestling promo, even when there were no cameras around and he didn't think anybody was listening. Burt was also strong as a bull—squat, deadlift, pick up cars, whatever. Total freak—and batshit crazy.

Our crew was actually well-hired, because with me being from town and every other guy being from one of the neighboring towns, any time things got out of hand, the odds were good that at least one of us would know at least one of the guys in the fight, and have a chance at talking them down.

So one night we were all at work, and the place was filled with these big, athletic farm guys who play hockey. The air was thick with testosterone and you could just tell that something was gonna happen. Adding to the potential for disaster was that Jay The Dick [aka Jay Reso, Adam's best friend; aka "Christian," Adam's WWE tag team partner] was also in the club, because there was really nowhere else to hang out in Orangeville.

I can't even remember what started it all, I just remember looking at the back corner and seeing fists start flying back there. Suddenly, it was like a tsunami of fists rolling toward us as more and more people got involved. By the time the wave crashed into us, there were at least thirty people fighting, which meant we could absolutely forget about stopping it. We just had to pick off guys one at a time and try to control it.

The first guy I grabbed started swinging at me, so I rammed him up against a support pillar to get a good hold of him and then began dragging him out. But a buddy of his came up from behind me and grabbed me in a chokehold, so now I'm not only fending off the choke, but the guy I had against the pillar is loose and he's getting ready to dial me in.

We were standing beside this kind of wooden barrier that ran around the dance floor, maybe four feet high and eighteen inches thick, and just as I was thinking I was finished, out of nowhere I saw The Dick running along the top of it. I pushed backward and slammed the guy behind me into a wall, which got me loose just as The Dick launched himself into the air, and a moment later—BOOM!—he hit the guy in front of me with a picture-perfect cross body block to the back! Slammed the guy face-first into the ground—I swear, you've never seen a better one in any wrestling ring than the one that The Dick pulled off that night.

L.   *From left to right: Wrestlers Zakk Wylde, Chi Chi Cruz, Jay "Christian" Reso (aka "The Dick") and Copeland circa 1995. Photo courtesy Adam Copeland.*

R.   *From left to right: Fraser "Baraka" Aitcheson, Adam, and me on the TV show SANCTUARY.*

To the best of my knowledge, that was the first-ever successful cross body block to be pulled off in a street fight—and don't even talk to me about that weak shit that [Chris] Jericho tried at that dive bar in Calgary, because it totally doesn't count if you don't connect.

> **Mauler's Note:** *See the "Lance Storm" chapter to find out what the hell Adam's talking about.*

Thankfully, the fight didn't last much longer, and we all came out of it more or less unscathed. Well, unscathed if you don't count having to listen to The Dick brag about how awesome he was for weeks afterward.

Male Stripper Night

If I fail to remember O'Toole's for any other reason, I will always remember it for the night that they featured male strippers. I was freaking out that I had to work that night, because I'd barely been to a female strip club at that point and I had no idea what the deal was gonna be.

The strippers arrived shortly after my shift started, and because it was the 90s, they were all mulletted out like crazy. Not that I can say anything about it since I was rockin' the same thing, plus my uniform was cowboy boots, jeans, and a white denim shirt, so I wasn't setting a very high fashion precedent.

After the show began, I stayed on the front door and tried to look back into the club as little as possible. But it was still my job to scan the room from time to time, and every time I did, it was like, "Whoa, shit, there's a dick." I didn't realize those guys were actually gonna get their shit right in the girls' faces and just SHAKE it. I don't know if that was legal, but it was sure goin' on.

Eventually I had to use the staff washroom, which was a tiny, single-user deal at the back. As I made my way back there, I tried to keep my eyes to the floor but it was like walking through dick land-mines the whole way. When I finally got to the back I let out a huge sigh of relief, little realizing I was about to open the unlocked bathroom door and find one of the peelers standing there wearing nothing but a cock ring! Porn magazine in one hand, junk in the other, going to TOWN on himself trying to get his shit hard.

At a young and impressionable seventeen years old, I didn't want to know about cock rings. What they were, what they were for, the whole process of getting 'em on—I didn't wanna know any of that. And I especially didn't want to be enlightened by a guy who was only too eager to explain it while simultaneously whacking his meat!

So, yeah... I witnessed that. And even with all the years that have passed and all the concussions I've suffered, I've still never found a way to un-know it.

For more Edge stories, get Adam Copeland on EDGE at:

a, *www.amazon.com*

🐦 *@EdgeRatedR*

Chapter Three

CHRIS 'HELLO KITTY' DAVIES

Photo courtesy Jenna Pozar.

"There were three semi-naked dudes crammed in there. It looked like the most fucked-up clown car ever!"

Access control was seldom a problem in the clubs that employed 3-time British Columbia's Strongest Man Chris "Hello Kitty" Davies, as he had little trouble obstructing entire doorways with his six-foot-two, three-hundred-ten-pound physique.

Boasting feats of Hulk-esque strength such as a 420+ lb. standing overhead barbell press, a 500+ pound raw bench press, a 780+ lb. raw-with-wraps squat, and a 720+ lb. raw, no-belt deadlift, the shockingly steroid-free Davies is an ever-increasing threat to take both the Canada's Strongest Man title and the pro strongman card on which he has set his sights.

Element

On New Year's Eve 2003, I was working on Georgia Street [in Vancouver] at a club called Element, which was attached to the Georgia Hotel. For some reason, the manager had pretty much exclusively booked East Indian parties that night, so the club was full of East Indian guys—and if you don't know Vancouver, I can tell you that even East Indian people themselves will verify that there's a lot of troublemakers in that group.

Just after the big countdown happened and everybody had their fun, a couple of guys who'd been sitting on one of the couches in the VIP section got into a big argument. It escalated FAST, and ended up with one of the guys breaking a champagne glass and stabbing the jagged stem into the other guy's eye! Kinda ruined the whole party.

Me and a couple of other bouncers grabbed the wounded guy, who had his hand clamped over his eye with blood streaming between his fingers. There was no bathroom inside Element—they shared one with the hotel—so we had to drag this poor guy out the back door and all the way through the hotel lobby leaving a trail of blood behind us!

When we finally got to the bathroom, we handed the guy a big wad of paper towels to press against the wound but they were saturated with blood almost immediately. We had to upgrade to bar towels just to keep up with the flow. When he was finally able to take his hand away from his face, all I could see was this giant skin-flap of an eyelid just hanging down over his cheek! The bottom part of the eyelid was completely slashed off and he had a nice, big gouge around his eye socket. It was such a mess that I couldn't even tell if his eye had been ruptured, and after the cops and paramedics came and got him, I never found out if he lost the eye or not.

One of the sickest parts of the story is that I worked there for another four months, and right up until the day I left they never bothered to clean up the big blood stain that poor dude left on the couch.

Bats In The Belfry… And In The Cellar

I went from there to a place called The Cellar, which was underground with a long staircase leading up to the front door.

One night a guy came in, and the first thing I noticed was that he was rockin' a pair of black Crocs. But whatever, we let him in because it was a slow night, and The Cellar didn't really have a dress code anyway. As soon as he got downstairs, though, he got into a yelling match with one of the bartenders and the bartender wanted him thrown out. Me and another bouncer named Tony tried talk the guy out, but we got the standard "Don't touch me, I know my rights" kind of stuff. So we finally said, "fuck it" and just grabbed an arm apiece.

As we dragged the guy backwards up the stairs, he was constantly trying to pull his arms free and swing at us, fighting us so hard that we could barely get him up the staircase. As we approached the top, I gave him a couple of hard knees to the side of the leg to settle him down, but that just made him worse. Then he pulled his legs up and started trying to climb over us and get back into the club, which would have meant falling all the way back down the staircase! That's when I knew that this guy was either crazy or on something.

He made it almost all the way over my shoulder, and I had to let go of his arm to keep him from falling. That gave him a free hand to crack me right in the forehead, and then I was SERIOUSLY pissed off. But I managed to keep from murdering him long enough for Tony and I to get him out to the street.

We plopped Crazy Guy down on the sidewalk and told him to get lost, but he still hadn't had enough and he squared off with me. By this point his Crocs had fallen off, so he bent down, picked one of them up, and tried to tomahawk-chop me on the forehead with it! (laughs) I just grabbed his wrist and peeled it out of his hand while Tony scooped the other Croc up off the pavement.

Davies loading a 400 lb. McGlashen Stone onto a four-foot-high platform. Ain't no thang. Photo courtesy Monte Arnold.

Then Tony looked at the guy and said, "Hey, do you like your Crocs?" and tore that shoe right in half, pulling the plastic top part away from the sole. Now it was like a flip-flop without the strap—just a "flop." I gave Tony the other shoe and he did the same thing to it before throwing the soles back to their owner. Then Crazy Guy lived up to his name by putting them both on the ground, stepping into them as if they were still intact, and trying to walk away with this confused expression on his face over why his shoes weren't coming with him! (laughs)

After he fucked off, we took the torn pieces of Croc and duct-taped them to the top of the door, leaving them as a warning to any other troublemaking Croc-wearers out there! (laughs)

Holland Kickboxer

A while later, St. Patrick's Day rolled around and we had to work on Sunday during the parade. Me and another doorman got there at noon, and we barely had the doors open before this Dutch guy came over from the hostel next door. When I asked for his ID, he said, "You don't need to see my fucking ID, just let me in."

We went back and forth for a minute before he finally said, "You don't know who I am. I'm one of the top Holland kickboxers." Then he backed up a few steps and started throwing spin kicks in the air, showing us how high he could kick. When we didn't react, he said, "What do you think of that?" and tried to slap me in the face!

Enough was enough. As he swung his hand I crouched down and speared him to the ground, taking out most of the velvet rope stands in the process. After I got him pinned I rolled him over face down, put one of his arms in a hammerlock, and then grabbed the length of velvet rope we were lying on and tied it around his upper body. He was lying there with his cheek squashed into the sidewalk and his arms pinned to his sides, yelling, "Let me up! You don't fight me on the ground, you fight me standing up! I am

Holland kickboxer!" (laughs) I told him, "Kickboxer, huh? Well, I guess jiu-jitsu won this time, didn't it?"

Now remember that this is the middle of the day on Sunday—the sun is out, people are getting out of church, and I'm already in a damn street fight! Finally a cop came by and looked down at us both, then looked at his watch and said, "Already? Are you serious?" He put the cuffs on the guy, but the dude started fighting the cop so they called a paddy wagon, and they needed three more cops to get this crazy dude into it. After the dust settled, one of the cops looked at the dude's passport and noticed that he was only three days into a one-year visa. THREE DAYS, and already getting arrested!

About a week later, that same cop walked by the club and I asked him about the crazy Dutchman. He said, "The guy started throwing a bunch of spin kicks in the lockup and we had to restrain him, so I decided to call immigration. After hearing the whole story they revoked his visa—he's already back in Holland!" (laughs)

(Pole) Smokin' In The Boys' Room

After that I moved over a few blocks to Davie Street, to a bar called Celebrities. It's a gay club, but it's known for being straight-friendly —on some nights it's almost all gay and on others it's really mixed.

We didn't have a staff washroom and had to use the public one, which meant always using a stall so nobody could attack you while you're vulnerable. One night I went in there to take a piss and opened one of the stall doors, then immediately wished that I hadn't. There were three semi-naked dudes crammed in there—it looked like the most fucked-up clown car ever! One dude was sitting on top of the toilet tank getting a blowjob, and the dude who was blowing him was getting fucked in the ass by the third dude! It was so overwhelming that I didn't even say a word—I just closed the door, turned around and went to find somewhere else to piss.

On another night, one of the bouncers started beckoning me toward the bathroom like there was a problem. I ran in there thinking there was a fight, but I found my co-worker standing outside one of the stalls and asking, "What do you think these guys are doing?" I'm thinking that there are guys in there doing drugs, but when I looked over the top of the stall, NOPE, no drugs, just two dudes buttfucking! Which really made me appreciate my co-worker calling ME over to deal with it. I pounded on the stall door and told 'em to break it up, and once they got their pants back on they left the club with no trouble.

At the end of the night, the other bouncer ran over to me holding up his phone and saying, "Hey, man—check it out!" Turned out that while I was kicking those two buttfuckers out, this guy was FILMING IT! And not just for a couple of seconds either—he had, like, THREE MINUTES of footage! And the guy was supposedly straight—or at least that's what he told us.

Creepy bastard.

🐦 *@ChrisStrongman*

Chapter Four

FRASER AITCHESON

All photos courtesy Fraser Aitcheson.

"I hear the sound of glass breaking and suddenly I'm lying on my side. I've just been thrown through the window of a taco place!"

My first experience with Fraser Aitcheson involved watching him lumber his scowling, muscle-bound self around Vancouver's late, lamented Olympic Gym and thinking that this was likely to be Olympic's next successful competitive bodybuilder.

But after dabbling in physique competition, Fraser went a different route, becoming a professional wrestler while working his way into the film/television industry.

Now a recognized, credentialed and established actor and stunt performer, Fraser's genetically-gifted physique (for which I've never stopped hating him) has made him a go-to guy for any stunt co-ordinator shooting a comic book or video game adaptation.

But before launching a career that includes portrayals of *Mortal Kombat: Legacy*'s "Baraka" and *Smallville*'s "The Persuader," he was just a young musclehead enforcing the rules (while breaking a few of them himself) in the bars and nightclubs of Vancouver.

Don't Yell at Strangers

In the late 80s, I worked at a club called Luvafair. I was really young, probably too young to even be working in that bar. One night a friend of mine comes running inside and she's like, "There's a bunch of guys beating up this dude, you gotta come outside and handle it!" Now, this is WAY before I knew how to fight or anything. I was just strong 'cause I was lifting monster weight every day, and I was also on a bunch of supplements that you can't buy at your local vitamin store.

So a few of us go out there, and there's this guy getting beaten up by like, four different dudes, so we save him and we break it up. Then the trash-talking commences, and the guys who were doing the beating start stepping to us. I end up squaring off with this one guy and he's really pushing it. I'm hearing from the peanut gallery behind me, "Knock him out! Knock him out!" and even the guy himself starts goading me, "Yeah, why don't you knock me out?" By this point, I feel like I have to do something to keep from losing face in front of all these other bouncers who I powerlift with.

So I grab the guy, pick him up over my head, slam him onto the hood of a car and start to feed him. Bang, bang, bang. He slides off the hood a little and sinks down, so I start giving him knees. Knees, knees, knees. I knee him to the point where his eye is almost hanging out—when I got home that night I threw my pants in the laundry, and the next morning my mom thought I got stabbed!

So I finally let the guy drop to the ground, at which point a couple of complete strangers, a guy and a girl, step off the curb and get right in my face. And when I say "in my face", I mean that their

Fraser as Baraka on the set of MORTAL KOMBAT: LEGACY.

faces are only inches away from mine. They're actually spraying spit on me while they're screaming, "WHAT ARE YOU DOING, YOU FUCKING ASSHOLE?" and whatever.

At that point, everything goes gray—I seriously don't remember a thing about what happens next. A minute later I come to and there's the guy and the girl lying on the street in front of me, both sleeping. I mean OUT COLD. So obviously, I must have dealt with them while I was blacked out.

It might sound weird to you, but I never feel bad when I tell that story, because I just don't have patience for that kind of thing. In a fight situation your adrenaline is flowing, your fight-or-flight instincts are on full blast, and you're just "go, go, go". At that moment, if some stranger is dumb enough to run up and start shrieking in your face, well... they get what they get.

If you don't like it, don't poke the monster with a stick.

Taco Time

A few years later, on one of my nights off, I go out with a bunch of friends to a club called Tonic on the Granville Street strip. We're having a good time, having drinks and stuff like that, but as we start to leave to go to the next club I get a weird feeling—like, hair standing up on the back of my neck. Then I realize, "Why aren't my friends with me?" and I turn around to see a circle forming in the crowd. A fight's starting and my friends are in it. Shit.

Because me and my friends are all bouncers, the Tonic bouncers let us get away with whatever, which means that nobody tries to break us up as the circle forms in front of the main bar. Our two groups square off, there's some yap-yap-yap, and then we all mutually decide to take it outside. At this point, the consensus is it's gonna be a one-on-one fight between the two guys who had the initial beef.

We go outside, and my one friend squares off with the one guy from their group and we're all watching. But then I have a problem. A BIG one. You see, before I left the house that night I had taken some, um, "supplements," and at that precise moment they hit me FULL BLAST like a bat across the face! Suddenly, I'm FUCKED.

But even through the haze, I can see that one of their guys is creeping up and trying to be the third man in. Now it looks like this fight's no longer going to be one-on-one, it's gonna be multiple-on-one. So I decide to intervene, and I kick off my sandals and intervene. Don't ask me why I'm wearing sandals to a nightclub because I have no idea, I just used to do stuff like that. I put my hands up, I jump in, and then... well, I don't really remember. Like I said, "supplements." A moment later I hear the sound of glass breaking all around me—PSSSSSH!—and suddenly I'm lying on my side.

I've just been thrown through the window of a taco place.

I'm like, "Holy fuck, I just got thrown through the window of the taco place! This is awesome!" But, really, not awesome. While I'm laying there I do a quick self-diagnostic to make sure there's no ar-terial bleeding or anything, and okay, there's not. Then I look up and see five pairs of legs—the dudes who threw me through the window are coming for me. Shit.

I cover up as they start laying the boots, but because there's so many guys involved I don't really get hurt. Unless guys really know what they're doing and can work as a group, they usually get in each other's way because they're all trying to get there at once. So they're all kicking and I weather, I weather, I weather, and a few bruises later there's finally a pause. So I pop right up to my feet and say "Alright, let's do it!"

They all stop and stare at me for a second... and then they take off! I guess they didn't expect me to be ready to go. Bitches. So I'm just standing there with nobody around—not even my damn *friends* are around—and now the cops are arriving and it's looking bad.

Then I see a couple of my friends spilling out of The Roxy across the street—I don't even know how they got over there so fast—and I'm PISSED. "Where the fuck were you?!" Excuses.

I quickly get out of there before the cops know who is who, and I go to a buddy's house to shower and get cleaned up. My shirt's ruined, so he gives me a shirt that says "INNOCENT BYSTANDER" on it—you know, so nobody will ever know I was involved. Half the fucking city saw me go through that window, there's even a little blood seeping through my clothes in various spots, but hey, with "Innocent Bystander" on my shirt it couldn't possibly be me, right? (laughs)

So we go back to Granville Street and hit The Roxy. We're drinking, and I'm telling the doormen the story when it just so happens that I see one of the guys who threw me through the window, sitting right there in the bar. I mention that fact to one of my friends, a pro boxer named Lumpy Dalton, and he asks me, "Are you sure that's the guy?" I'm like, "Well... I'm PRETTY sure that's the guy..." but that's good enough for Lumpy and off he goes. Shit.

I start telling the doormen that something's about to go down, but I don't even get halfway through what I'm saying before Lumpy taps the guy on the shoulder:

"Hey, you're one of the guys who threw that dude through the window, right?"

"Yeah..."

SMASH. With a fucking PINT MUG.

And then Lumpy goes to work.

All the bouncers rush in as Lumpy proceeds to kill this guy, and at that point I decide that I've had enough and I ghost out the door. From what I heard the next day, Lumpy's victim ended up with stitches, while Lumpy walked away clean after the bouncers smuggled him out the back door.

Solid motherfucker, that Lumpy.

Chapter Five

ENSON 'YAMATO DAMASHII' INOUE

Photo courtesy Susumu Nagao.

"I grabbed the guy and started dragging him into the back, and the security guys came running, yelling, 'We're sorry! We're sorry!'"

During the 1990s heyday of Japan's SHOOTO mixed martial arts group, the American-born Enson "Yamato Damashii" Inoue reigned as its heavyweight king.

A volatile and controversial character (to this day he remains an unapologetic organized crime associate), Brazilian jiu-jitsu black belt Inoue helped to spearhead the rise of Japanese MMA through classic clashes with the likes of Frank Shamrock, Randy "The Natural" Couture, and NCAA wrestling champion Royce Alger.

But he is best remembered for one of the gutsiest performances in MMA history—a swing-for-the-fences, "go home on your shield" loss to Ukranian juggernaut Igor Vovchanchyn that stands as a prime example of what the words "fighting spirit" really mean.

Inoue retired from MMA never having submitted in a single fight. During recent years he has turned his energy to charitable works, and in 2013 he completed a walk across Japan to raise money for those affected by the 2011 tsunami and Fukushima nuclear reactor meltdown.

Gangster Fight

I recently got in the middle of a situation at an MMA show called RINGS: The Outsider. It's a group run by a famous wrestler named Akira Maeda, and a lot of Yakuza [Japanese organized crime figures] fight on those shows.

Maeda's organization got a reputation as being kind of crazy because a lot of the guys who fought there didn't understand it was a sport, and so things would become personal. A guy would be watching his brother getting pummeled in the ring, and he'd take it personal and then things would happen outside the ring. You can't have that, because if it happens too much then the police just shut the event down.

I would get paid just to be at these shows because I've got a lot of connections with the gangsters and the Yakuza people. Because of the respect they have for me, they usually try to control themselves to a point where they don't riot or anything like that.

One night I was at a show and after one of the fights, the guy who won stood over his opponent a little bit longer than he should have and screamed down at him. But nothing physical happened as they left the ring, so I thought everything was okay and I just sat there waiting for the next fight to start.

Then all these big security guys came up to me and said that there was some shit going down in the back. Which struck me as weird, because I was like, "You guys are security, why the fuck are you telling me?" (laughs) But then I realized that if they're coming to me, there's probably some crazy-ass riot going on with gangsters who aren't gonna be listening to the security guards.

So I walked into the back, and sure enough there was the two [Yakuza] fighters squared off with each other, and none of the security guards wanted to get involved. So I stepped in between the two guys, and even though they were both going crazy, they at least calmed down a little bit when they saw me. You could see them start to control their anger a little more. Then I noticed that the official security guys weren't even standing with me to have my back—I'm just standing there between these two guys who have all their friends behind them, and the security staff is completely out of it!

Now, the usual idea would be to separate the guys involved, but I did things different. The way things go in the gangster world, if shit goes down then you have to settle it *now*. If you're gonna hurt each other, if you're gonna solve it, you have to do it now. Because if you let it go and it goes through the [Yakuza] families, then even if the higher-up guys decide everything's cool, you might still have the lower guys hurting each other. You don't know who's gonna tell what family member, and who's gonna run into who. The whole problem can escalate, get out of hand.

So I took the two [fighters] in a room, just me and them. They were still worked up to the point where they looked like they were gonna throw down, but if they did it in there it would be cool [because it was] just two guys. No weapons, no friends are gonna jump in, it's just us. They kept yelling for a while and then the guy who lost the fight started crying—like, angry crying. But at the same time, [he] seemed to be more sad than pissed off. I guess those guys used to be friends, and he was sad that the other dude had disrespected him.

At that point I said, "Okay, this is cool—it's better that I'm not here so you guys can sort this out," and I stepped out of the room. When the security guys saw me come out alone and close the door, they said, "What the fuck are you doing? Why aren't you in there?!" (laughs) But there were no knives or weapons in that room, just some lockers and some chairs, and how much damage are you really going to do to each other with chairs?

The security guys tried to go in there but I stopped them because... you know how sometimes when there's people around trying to stop it, a guy will get braver? You know, he says shit that he probably wouldn't say if it was just him and the guy he's mad at, all alone. Sometimes having a crowd around can turn a mouse into a lion. But with just them alone in a room, there was no pride involved and it could come down to what the issue was really all about.

I listened through the door and I heard yelling from both guys, then it turned to crying, then the crying turned to talking, and after that everything got resolved. Hmmm... I guess this would be a better story if somebody got stabbed! (laughs)

Because of the respect I have with these underworld figures, I've gotten really good at getting people to talk instead of go to war. Which is actually really funny, because back in the day I [was the first guy to] jump up and say, "Let's fuckin' take it outside!" (laughs) The first option I used back then is the last one that I want to use today. The way I do things now, problems get sorted out and nobody has to get hurt.

Bouncer Attitude

Japanese people really like to hire black bouncers. I'm not sure why—maybe because they think those guys look mysterious and tough. Because guys like Mike Tyson are black, and Japanese people see them as the ultimate tough guys. I don't know, but whatever the reason is, Japanese people like to hire black bouncers.

Some of those guys come in and they believe that image, they've got an attitude about them being bad-asses. Not all of 'em, of course, but some of 'em. And those guys can really create problems.

At [fight] shows I always have an all-access pass, but I went to one show where I hadn't collected my pass yet and the guard didn't recognize me. He came up and stopped me, and I explained, "My name's Enson, I just have to collect my pass." But he kept giving me attitude, you know? Like he was this big bad-ass or something. So I let it go and let it go, just trying to get my pass—but finally the switch went on and "Old Enson" came out! (laughs)

I grabbed the guy and started dragging him into the back [of the arena], and then all the other security guys came running over. They didn't wanna touch me, but they were all saying, "We're sorry! We're sorry!" and explaining to the black guy who I am and that I was supposed to be there. Man, so many times security guys think that throwing attitude at you is going to solve the problem, but you can't have an attitude like that.

It's like when I'm acting as a mediator [for Yakuza disputes], I don't walk in there with a chip on my shoulder. So much fucking hormone is going on, you don't need another third-party hormone because it's only gonna mix in a bad way. Sometimes security guys think that throwing attitude around is going to solve the problem—and sometimes, yeah, a scary guy will deter you from doing shit—but when the shit hits the fan and you're pissed off and you just wanna fuck someone up, no big dude is gonna turn that off.

If they come at you with attitude then, they're just gonna fuel the fire.

🐦 *@EnsonInoue*

Chapter Six

PAT 'THE CROATIAN SENSATION' MILETICH

Photo courtesy Zack Lynch (MMAPhotography.com).

"All around us it's baseball bats and knuckles and Jai-alai paddles flying everywhere—CHAOS!"

I'm going to have to keep this description of UFC Hall-of-Famer Pat "The Croatian Sensation" Miletich short, because if I enumerate every awesome thing that he has accomplished, this entry will be ten pages long!

A lifelong wrestler, Pat entered the sport of MMA in the mid-90s, and through numerous victories in no-weight-limit fights he quickly cemented his status as one of the baddest dudes to come out of the American midwest.

His rise continued all the way to the UFC, where he notched five world championship victories between 1998 and 2001 (six if you count a four-man tournament at UFC's Ultimate Japan event in Tokyo).

Today, he works as a highly sought-after ring/cageside commentator, and remains one of the most successful and respected trainers in the history of his chosen sport.

But before racking up all of those victories and accolades, Pat Miletich was just a hard-headed bouncer trying to keep the peace in the roadhouses and nightclubs of his native Iowa.

Riot at Little Joe's

Back in the early 90s, I was working with two other bouncers at a club whose name I forget—it was up on the hill in Davenport, on Harrison Street. The place was owned by a guy named Little Joe, who also owned a bunch of strip clubs in the area. For some reason, Joe thought it would be a good idea for this particular club that I was working at to have a hip-hop night.

Now, I warned him against it because there was a lot of gang activity in the area and I figured there'd be a lot of fights and stuff. But he went on ahead with his idea, and his first hip-hop night took place a short time later during a massive snowstorm.

Sure enough, a bunch of gang-bangers rolled in from nearby Rock Island [Illinois]—which we used to call "Little Chicago"— along with some other bad guys from Davenport. Pretty soon the place was packed, and me and the other two bouncers were the only white guys in the joint.

It didn't take long before some rival gangs got into it, and of course the three of us had to dive in to try to break it up. But the crowd didn't take too kindly to some white boys trying to break up their fight, and so they all joined forces against us! After it started, I had no idea what was happening to the other bouncers because I was totally preoccupied with fending for myself.

Right away I got clamped in a side headlock by somebody, which actually ended up working in my favor because the guy's head was pressed against mine and was protecting me on that side. A lot of the guys were wearing their coats inside, so I was able to fight back by grabbing them by their jackets, pulling them in, and putting their head on one side of mine with the headlock-guy's head still pressed against the other. That protected me on both sides and kept anybody from getting clean shots on me.

While I was holding these guys by the jacket, I'd pull their lapel across their throat and choke them unconscious with it. Then I'd drop them, grab another guy, and repeat the process. I left a trail of four or five bodies as I worked my way toward the door, with the dummy who was headlocking me never realizing that he was helping me the whole time. When I finally got to the door, I slid backwards out of the headlock and snatched the guy in a standing rear choke, then backed outside while using him as a human shield.

In spite of the giant snowstorm, a bunch of the gang-bangers were already outside, waiting to jump on any bouncer who made it out of the club. I kept my head down as they swarmed me, and I dragged my guy out to the middle of the street by which point he'd gone completely limp. Just as I was just letting him slide out of my arms, someone came up on my blind side and smashed me in the side of the head with a brick! Lucky for me I instinctively managed to roll with it, and even though it put a pretty good lump on my head it didn't hurt me too bad. The guy even yelled out "YEAH!!!" I guess thinking that a shot that solid would put me down. But when I just turned around and looked at him, his jaw dropped like he'd seen a damn ghost! (laughs) He didn't even have time to raise his hands as I rifled a straight right into his face, and he was still collapsing to the pavement when three squad cars came flying up the street.

The cops barely managed to get out of their cruisers before the crowd had them and me completely surrounded, and at that point I realized that I was the only bouncer who'd even made it out of the club. So it was just me, five cops and three German Shepherds standing in an outward-facing circle, surrounded by swirling snow and a hundred screaming, cussing people trying to attack us from all sides.

Somehow, we managed to hold them off until enough additional cops arrived to get things under control. To this day I still think about how ugly that scene could have gotten, but thankfully the other two bouncers ended up being okay, and I went home with nothing worse than a big lump on the side of my head.

Pool Party War

A while later I went to a big house party at a buddy's place in an up-scale area of Davenport that we called "The Heights." Really wealthy families living in big mansions, stuff like that. The house had a big pool out back and we spent the day lounging around it, drinking and swimming and whatever.

In the late afternoon, this one dummy decides he wants to start a fight. Now, even though me and my friends are not officially boun-cing at this party, we still consider ourselves responsible for keeping any idiots from spoiling the fun. So one of my buddies beats the guy up pretty good, and the guy gets in his car and leaves. Within minutes we've forgotten about the whole thing, and we continue on for a few more hours until things wind down to just me and four guys drinking beer in the garage.

It's just starting to get dark when two cars come tearing up the street and screech to a stop in front of the house. I hear a bunch of car doors slamming, and then I see nine guys holding baseball bats and marching up the driveway! Right away, one of my buddies jumps up and hits the switch to close the garage door, and the rest of us start looking around for stuff to help us even the odds.

There's a couple of those big wicker Jai-alai paddles hanging on wall pegs, so two guys immediately grab those. Now that I think of it, that might have been a world record for the first time Jai-alai equipment was used in a street fight! (laughs) I pick up a pitchfork out of the corner, the other guys arm up with whatever they can find, and then I say, "Okay, open the door!"

The door opens and we walk right out. The nine guys start backing down the driveway a little, which gives us the high ground because the driveway's on an angle. Since I'm in the front, I start lunging and feinting with the pitchfork at the two guys closest to me. Those dumb bastards are standing so close together that they can't even swing their baseball bats without hitting each other, so I keep jabbing at them until I have the timing and distance the way I want them. Then I drop the pitchfork—because I'm not looking to commit murder here—and I launch myself at them and clothesline them both to the ground.

I land on top and start pounding them both, but right away I feel one guy get ripped out from underneath me and lifted up. I look up to see my buddy Wally—who's an incredibly strong guy, around my size but a lot thicker—picking this guy up and dumping him right on his head. The guy's knocked out immediately but Wally starts punting him anyway, and all around us it's baseball bats and knuckles and Jai-alai paddles flying everywhere—CHAOS!

Wally's still punting his guy when another dork runs up and swings a bat at Wally's midsection. But Wally just lifts up his arm and flexes his lat muscle, and the bat bounces right off Wally's lat! He takes the damn thing like it's nothing, and then he hits the guy with a right hand and knocks him clean out.

By now I've finished my guy and moved on to another. I've got the new guy down on the ground, and I'm beating the shit out of him when he starts screaming, "MY LEGS! MY LEGS!", which is kind of puzzling because I've been punching him in the face. But then I look over my shoulder and see the smallest and craziest of my buddies, a guy named Greg Bates—we used to call him "Master" Bates—laughing this crazy laugh and stabbing the guy in the legs with the pitchfork! Not just poking the guy, mind you—STABBING him. I have to reach over and snatch the damn pitchfork out of Greg's hands to keep him from killing the guy!

A minute later, only one of their guys is still conscious, and he's crawling on his hands and knees in the middle of the street while me, Wally, and a guy named Bob Franks are taking turns kicking him in the head. He's finally fading into Dreamland when I notice colored lights moving over his body, and I look up to see squad cars racing up the street toward us.

The cops come skidding up and it's like a war zone—bleeding, unconscious bodies all over the place with baseball bats, pitchforks and Jai-alai paddles scattered everywhere. One of the cops looks around for a minute, and then looks at me and asks what happened.

But at that moment, all the beer in my stomach combines with the huge adrenaline dump I'm experiencing, and instead of answering I just vomit all over the sidewalk! (laughs)

Thankfully, the police end up accepting our side of the story, and my friends and I all get off scott-free. As the cops call for a couple of ambulances to clean up the bodies, me and my buddies decide to call it a night and head home.

Good party. (laughs)

Tommy Hernandez

This one's an off-duty story about me and a buddy named Tommy Hernandez. Tommy was an Illinois state wrestling champion and he

Pat accepting the first-ever National Wrestling Hall of Fame George Tragos Award from legendary world & Olympic champion Dan Gable (with WWE Hall of Famer Mick Foley looking on). Photo courtesy Joyce Paustian.

was also funnier than shit. One year MTV had a nationwide contest to find a new VJ, and Tommy took second place but I swear he should have won. Tommy's absolutely hilarious.

So me and Tommy go out to this place called The Blue Flamingo—yeah, I know it sounds like a gay bar but it's not. The bouncers know us so they let us in the back door, and we walk past a bunch of people playing foosball to get some beers at the back bar.

While we're standing there drinking, a guy walks away from one of the tables and comes up to us. He says, "Hey, I'm trying to play foosball here. This tournament's for a lot of money and you guys are distracting me. You gotta get the fuck out of here." But I say, "We're twenty feet away from you and we're not bothering anybody. Just play your damn game."

Now he's pissed, but what's he gonna do? He goes back to his table and ends up losing the game, after which of course he freaks out. He storms off to the bathroom to collect himself, but when he comes back you can tell that he's still steaming mad.

So Tommy nudges me with his elbow and says, "Watch this," and then he beckons to the guy to come over to us. The guy walks over and says "What?!" and Tommy goes, "Hey... ya fuckin' lost, didn't ya?" (laughs)

The guy loses his mind even worse, and he goes off to tell the bar owner on us. Turns out that he and the owner are buddies, so the owner comes back with the guy and says, "I'm sorry, Pat, but you guys gotta go—your buddy's causing problems with my friends. No disrespect, but you gotta go." I tell him, "That's bullshit! There's no way we're leaving," and shortly after that we're surrounded by several bouncers, as well as the owner who's being an asshole and the foosball guy who's now gloating his ass off.

As we're all standing there, Tommy slowly looks around from face to face until he finally lands on the owner.

"So," Tommy says. "You're 100% sure we have to leave."

"Yeah, I'm 100% sure."

"Let me get this straight—there is no fucking way that we're gonna be able to stay in this bar tonight."

"Sorry, there's no way."

"Alright... I'm gonna try this one more time. There is *nothing I can say* to convince you to let us stay in this bar tonight. We absolutely *have* to leave, right?"

"That's right, you have to leave. No way around it."

Tommy ponders this for a second, looks over at me, smiles, and then SMOKES the foosball guy right in the face! (laughs)

The guy's instantly unconscious and it's on. I'm grabbing bouncers by the hair and throwing them around, Tommy's doing whatever he's doing, and we're just tearing the place apart. It goes on for a minute or two until there's a pause in the action, and I look up to see two giant bouncers marching toward the door carrying Tommy on their shoulders.

Still smiling as he goes past, Tommy looks back at me and yells:

"HEY, PAT! I GUESS WE'RE LEAVIN'!" (laughs)

Chapter Seven

'FRANKY THE MOBSTER'

Photo courtesy Marc-André Boulanger.

"She has three shots of cognac to start her day—but if your job is sucking some dirty old man's cock, of course you need something to get through it."

If you're a pro wrestler who has worked anywhere in Eastern Canada (or if you know someone who has), then you've at least heard of pro wrestler/actor Marc-André Boulanger aka "Franky the Mobster."

A longstanding veteran of the Québec independent wrestling scene, the eye-bulging, vein-popping, hypermuscular "FTM" is respected for both his in-ring legacy and his all-the-time intensity.

Certain figures inspire fear and affection in equal measure, and the more I learned about Franky, the more I found him to be one of those guys. By all accounts a great dude, but do NOT fuck with him.

Pretty much every friend of Franky's who I told of my intention to interview him just laughed, shook their head, and said that they couldn't wait to hear what he told me. After this interview was over, I completely understood why.

WARNING: This is EXTREMELY NSFW.

The Body Shop

A few years ago, I got a job working the day shift at what I was told was a strip joint called The Body Shop in Saint-Antoine, Québec. My first impression was that it looked like a shithouse. Looking at it from the outside, I figured I would just have some drunken-ass, ugly strippers to watch over during the day, and then go on with my night.

The place had a reputation, but I didn't know how bad it really was till I got there. On my first day, the manager brings me over and says, "Okay, let me show you the booths." They were like your everyday strip joint booths, except that he points and says, "You see those lights in the booths? If you ever see the cops out front, you press the button up by the front desk to activate those lights, and warn the girls to stop what they're doing and go back to the locker room. The lights also go on downstairs where we have three rooms that the customers can rent if they want."

That's the first notice I got that I was actually working in a whorehouse.

My first day there, one of the girls walks in at 11 AM. She's maybe four-foot-nine, and right away she has three shots of cognac to start her day. That surprised even me, but then I thought that if your job is sucking some dirty old man's cock, of course you need something to get through it.

Another one of the broads had to be at least 45 years old, and botoxed all the way to her teeth. She looked like that old rich broad that you see on the news, the one who's had too many surgeries and looks like a monster. This chick looked like that, plus her tits had to be at least twenty pounds each. Just a disaster.

At the front desk, I had a monitor attached to a camera that was pointed at the parking lot. I could see the cement stairs leading up to the front door, which couldn't be opened from the outside unless I pressed a button. It was like an airlock, you came through the front door into a little room and there was a second door that led to the club. If one door was open, the other one would not unlock, so they had things sewn up pretty tight in this place.

On my first day, I was looking at my monitor and I saw this old man coming up to the door who had to be three hundred fifty pounds on a five-foot-eight frame. Ugly old man, looked like your typical pervert out of a movie. I let him in and he walked up to the counter and wanted to shake my hand.

Now, my take on bouncing has always been that I'm not there to be a dick. I hate when you walk into a place and the bouncer has that "I'm a bouncer" face, it's stupid. The bouncer's often the first person to have contact with a customer, so in my mind that means you gotta be polite. So I shook.

The four girls on duty came out to greet the customer, and right away three of them said, "FUCK THAT" and powdered straight back to the locker room. But the one with the face, she stuck around, and the old guy paid to go downstairs with her.

While they were down there, the other girls came out and asked me, "Do you know him?", and I said, "It's my first fucking day, how am I gonna know this guy?" Then they all started laughing like something's funny.

I looked at the monitor and saw the guy's car, it was a huge fucking Mercedes, and I said, "Look at his car, the guy must be loaded. Why didn't you take him?" The short chick said, "When he's done, go check the room", and then they all walked away laughing their asses off.

Maybe twenty minutes later, the old dude came back upstairs covered in sweat. It was leaking through his clothes—on his back, under his pits, on his front—and he was breathing hard, panting, like HENNNNH, HENNNNH, while keeping his eyes down to the floor. He didn't say a word on his way out, he just shook my hand again which is something that I thoroughly regret to this day. Shortly after that, the bitch with the face came up looking as casual as if she had just served him breakfast—which is kind of what she did.

Wanting to know what the girls were laughing about, I went downstairs to the room which was really kinky and gross with red lights and a heart-shaped bed covered in leather. I looked in and spotted something on the bed, but I couldn't make it out with the red lights. So I turned on the regular lights and...

There was shit all over the bed.

SHIT.

I just stood there, staring like a fucking moron because I couldn't believe it. I probably said twenty times to myself, "It's SHIT!... It's SHIT!...", like I had Tourette's or something.

When the shock wore off and I could finally move again, I went straight to the janitor's closet to grab some industrial-strength cleaner, and I dumped the whole bottle out on the bed. I didn't care if I screwed up the leather—it was covered in shit anyway so how was I gonna ruin it worse? As quick as I could, I cleaned up the mess and threw away every towel that I used, and then I came upstairs, steaming mad.

The girls were still laughing but they shut up quick when they saw my face. I looked at them and said, "WHERE IS SHE?", and they pointed at the back room. I went and found the old broad and said, "I was hired to provide security. I was not hired to clean up SHIT!" But as angry as I was, I was also curious—I had to know exactly what happened. So I asked her, "Which one of you shat?! Who shat?!"

She said, "Well, that's what he likes—he likes it when I shit on his face! He pays me good!" And now I am losing it. "Fine!", I said. "Shit all you want—but if I have to clean it up ever again, I swear on my dad and mother that I am gonna grab you by the hair and stick your fucked-up face right in it, you fuckin' repulsive whore!"

Then she actually had the nerve to say, "You can't talk to me like that!", as if there's a manual of how I'm supposed to talk to hookers with fucked-up faces who shit in guys' mouths!

From then on, every time that elephant-hippopotamus motherfucker came in, he was the one customer whose hand I would never shake. He ended up dying a few months later— maybe from shit poisoning, I don't know.

Little Mike

On another night, this guy came into the bar who they called Little Mike because he was five-foot-five-ish and about a buck forty. He was either a striker or supporter of one of the local bike clubs, which can sometimes be a problem but Little Mike was actually a nice guy. He was in the bar for about four hours and he went downstairs twice with different girls, but after the second time he came back up all aggravated. He was screaming at one of the strippers, "You fuckin' cunt! You fuckin' whore!" So I went over and said, "Whore, yes, that's her job. So what's the problem?" He said, "She stole my fuckin' money!"

If any of the other girls were involved, I would have believed the customer right away. But the problem here was that he was mad at the one chick in the whole place who I would never believe would steal. I had gotten to know this girl and I was certain that she'd never fuck with a guy's money. She'd fuck him FOR money, but never WITH his money.

So I told the guy, "Brother, you need to calm down", but he kept going nuts, like, "Fuck you! Don't you know who I am?!!" I said, "Well, from the fact that you asked me that, I know that you're nobody. If you were really somebody, first of all I would already know, and second of all, you wouldn't feel the need to say that. You would just leave here and then I would be in trouble."

That really made him crazy. He spilled his booze on the bar, kicked a chair over, and stuck his hand down his pants like he was going for a piece. So much for talking. I clocked him in the face and then grabbed his shirt with both hands. [In] the part of the bar we were in, the ceiling was only seven feet high, and without even thinking I lifted his little ass up and rammed his head through the ceiling. Then I dropped him back down, punched him again, got him in a full nelson, and drove him facedown to the ground. By that point

I was so full of adrenaline that I accidentally squeezed too hard, and I felt his shoulders popping as I rubbed his face on the floor.

Now, I have to stop for a second and tell you that I hate violence. I did not want that to happen. But I also know that you can't mess around in a situation like that, where you might be about to lose your life. Later on I would find out that he didn't even have a fucking gun, but hey, how would I know that at the time?

I dragged him over to the doorway and opened the first of the two doors by slamming his face into it. But when I got to the second door and did the same thing, I was unaware that some of the customers were holding the first door open. Remember how I told you that both doors can't be open at the same time? Yeah, not good.

You could actually hear his nose explode against the second door. Fuck. Now I'm holding this bloody-faced little asshole as I turn around to the customers and say, "Would you be so kind as to get the FUCK back and close the door?" When they did that and I finally got the front door open, I threw him down the cement stairs and the noises he made were not very nice.

Still shaking, I took a big breath and went over to the bar to get a triple Jack and Coke to take the edge off. Then I went over and looked on the monitor, and breathed a sigh of relief when I saw that the guy was back on his feet and getting into his truck. Okay, he's going home now, right?

Nope.

Once he was in the driver's seat, the crazy fuck gunned the engine and plowed straight into the cement staircase, trying to drive up it and into the front door! But it was a steep staircase so he didn't make it, and instead he bounced off to the side and straight into where

MY truck was parked! Smashed my doors right in! Then he backed up and did it a second time, and smashed my truck again! Now my truck is FUCKED. I was losing it, and I ran outside just as he gunned it out of the parking lot and into traffic, straight across one of the busiest streets in town. It was a miracle he didn't hit someone.

As I watched him drive away and looked at my ruined truck, I suddenly realized that almost the entire staff and many of the patrons had come out behind me to see what was going down. And of course, the last person out let the door close behind them, which locked automatically, and I don't have my key or my phone.

I'm gonna kill these girls.

Ten minutes later, the bartender finally realized what happened and opened the door to let us all in. About an hour later, the phone rang and it was for me, and on the other end it's the fucking guy! He's almost crying as he says:

"Look, man, I'm sorry. I was angry, but I'm sorry. Now can I please come back and have a drink?"

Jesus Christ.

🐦 *@frankytm*

Chapter Eight

GLENN ENNIS

All photos courtesy Glenn Ennis.

"Still holding onto the crazy bitch, he reared his head back and coco-bonked her right in the noggin!"

As a three-time member/two-time captain of Canada's world cup rugby team and a member of several international all-star teams, Glenn Ennis is arguably the greatest rugby player ever produced by "The Great White North." In 1991, he became one of the first five foreign-born players to sign a professional contract in the Japanese Rugby League, where he became fluent in Japanese while playing eight seasons with the 1995 champion Suntory team.

After returning to his native Vancouver, Ennis turned his hand to the entertainment industry, where he has worked on over seventy movies and TV shows as an actor, stuntman and stunt coordinator, doubling stars such as Steven Seagal, Ray "The Punisher" Stevenson, Jason Momoa and WWE superstars Edge and Triple H.

Systems

During the 80s, I worked at a downtown Vancouver club called Systems. [It was] kind of a poser place—lots of collars turned up in there, shiny shirts and baggy pants, stuff like that. When a fracas broke out, it was usually limited to pushing and shoving because nobody wanted to get their clothes and hair messed up.

One night, a few guys got into it with us and we hustled them all out into the alley behind the club. It was the usual pushing and shoving and scuffling and "I'll kill you," so basically not anything to be concerned about. However, since we were outnumbered seven to five, it was taking a while to get things under control.

Finally, the girlfriend of one of the guys we were fighting started to pipe up and get more animated, and she quickly became a serious problem. Slapping at guys over people's shoulders, screaming in people's faces, basically revving everyone up in the way that only a girl can when there's a bunch of guys whose testosterone is peaking.

One of our bouncers, a two-hundred-eighty-pound bodybuilder named Ray Nelson, ended up holding her off with one hand while clutching a fistful of one guy's shirt with the other. At that point, she got louder and more violent than ever, so while still hanging onto the guy, Ray wrapped his free arm around the chick's neck and pulled her down into a headlock.

Well, if she'd been a problem before, she was completely out of control now. Kicking Ray in the shins, punching his balls, reaching up to pull his ponytail—a ponytail that was perfectly okay for a man to have back then, because remember, it was the 80s.

Ray weathered the storm as long as he could, but when she started clawing at his eyes with her nails, he finally lost it. Still holding onto the crazy bitch, he reared his head back and brought it down HARD, coco-bonking her right in the noggin! Pretty astounding when you consider the logistics, because Ray was so musclebound that his joints barely bent.

Glenn in full "Seagal Mode."

Unsurprisingly, she went down like a sack of potatoes. Ray was gentle, mind you, and he cradled her lovingly in the crook of his free arm as he lowered her to the pavement and leaned her against the wall.

The loud KLUNK of the heads and the abrupt stoppage of the chick's incessant screaming got the immediate attention of everyone in the alley, and all the air instantly went out of the fight. Nobody knew how to process the shock and awe of what they'd just seen, and suddenly those seven wannabe tough guys were as docile as sheep.

The whole thing was so startlingly effective that for months afterward, we would joke that any time a fight broke out we should just punch the nearest girl in the head! (laughs)

No. 5 Orange

I also did a stint at a legendary Vancouver strip joint called the No. 5 Orange. Had to fight my way through more than a few customers back then, but at six-foot-four and a fit 220, I usually had no trouble. Especially considering that everybody was usually so drunk and stupid that whatever fighting skills they had were drastically diminished.

A huge guy named Nick Hebeler, who played defensive end for the BC Lions, used to come in with one of his teammates who everybody called "Yaz." I think his real name was "Yazanowski" or something. Both of them were around the same size, roughly six and a half feet tall and over 280 pounds.

Hebeler was kind of a kook. He used to wear these shiny orange shoes and shave his hair into the shape of an arrow pointing forward, telling people, "That's the way I'm goin' and nobody's stoppin' me!" In other words, probably not a guy who came up on an academic scholarship.

One night, Hebeler and Yaz decided to walk behind the bar and throw the bartender out of there, then start pouring unlimited shots for themselves and the other customers. My heart sank as I realized that I was expected to put a stop to it to justify my nine dollars an hour. So I screwed up my courage and went to have a chat with the Mutant Brothers. But I only got as far as, "Hey guys, would you mind..." before they turned around, stabbed their hot dog-sized fingers in my direction, and yelled "GET THE FUCK OUT!"

At that moment, all my years of bouncing experience came to bear. Faced with nearly six hundred pounds of angry brawn, I looked both guys up and down, calculated their potential weaknesses, formulated a strategy... and then turned on my heel and walked away. Sometimes, truly efficient bouncing consists of letting the fucking manager deal with it! (laughs)

Doubling Ray Stevenson in
PUNISHER: WAR ZONE.

The Roxy

A few years later, I was working occasional shifts at The Roxy on Granville Street [in downtown Vancouver]. I wasn't on duty when this story happened, just putting in a few extracurricular hours at the bar.

I was sitting on a barstool and chatting up some honey when I felt someone kicking the leg of my stool. I looked up to see this guy standing over me, saying, "That seat's taken." I said, "Yeah, by me" and turned back around. Two seconds later, a full-force sucker punch hit me right in the temple—not enough to put me away, but more than enough to hurt like hell. I immediately jumped off my stool, and not-so-immediately turned around, giving the asshole plenty of time to drift me four more times in various spots on my melon.

Understandably pissed, I finally got the guy lined up and smashed my fist straight into his face. Down he went, just in time for a buddy of his to jump in. So I smashed that guy too, and down *he* went—both of them laying there, looking very confused about why the room was suddenly sideways.

At that point the bouncers arrived—all of them friends of mine, of course—and I pointed at the floor and said, "These guys gotta go!" The carcasses were dragged away as I put my overturned barstool back in place and sat down.

But as I sat there with my head throbbing, I got angrier and angrier. That dick had nailed me five times in the head, and I only got to hit those guys one time each! It was definitely not enough.

With steam shooting out of my nostrils, I went outside to see if they were still around, and lo and behold there they were, wide awake and standing right outside the front door. They both spotted me right away—not a hard thing to do, I'll admit.

Dickface #1: "I'm gonna sue your ass for assau…!"

Boom.

Dickface #2: "Hey!"

Boom.

Both of them back on the ground, and this time you could practically see the Tweety birds circling their heads.

Then came my glorious crowning moment. Feeling like the toughest bastard on Granville Street, I took a step backward and my heel caught the curb. Over I went, onto my tailbone on the concrete, and that was the exact moment that I learned the truth in something I'd heard on a nature program about how adrenaline causes animals to void their bowels.

In other words, I crapped my pants on impact.

After an awkward moment of looking around to see if anyone had heard any tell-tale noises, I got up, duck-walked back into the club, and waddled a beeline straight to the staff washroom where I performed the delicate extraction and self-sanitization procedure.

I feel really sorry for whoever had to empty the garbage that night.

---

www.GlennEnnisStunts.com

Chapter Nine

'JUDO' GENE LeBELL

Photo courtesy Hans Gutknecht.

"I turned to him and said, 'Next time, I wanna take the pictures and YOU can hold onto the naked guy!'"

If ever a man deserved the nickname of "The Toughest Man Alive," it's actor, stuntman, martial artist and pro wrestler "Judo" Gene LeBell. A master of catch-as-catch-can wrestling and a two-time American judo champion (1954-55), LeBell has spent over seventy years learning from and teaching some of the greatest fighters in history.

In 1963, LeBell won the first-ever televised mixed martial arts bout, choking out middleweight boxer Milo Savage in Salt Lake

City, Utah. He went on to teach groundfighting techniques to the legendary Bruce Lee, and referee the historic 1976 Muhummad Ali vs. Antonio Inoki match in Tokyo, Japan.

Also a former motorcycle tester for Honda and a veteran of over 1000 film, TV and commercial productions, LeBell can be frequently seen in the corner of Olympic judo bronze medalist and first-ever female UFC champion "Rowdy" Ronda Rousey (see picture).

A godfather of mixed martial arts and a personal hero of mine, "Judo Gene" rolls into his eighties as a venerated trainer, cageside judge, and figurehead for stunt performers, pro wrestlers, martial artists, and garden-variety tough bastards the world over.

The Olympic Auditorium

Back in the late forties or early fifties—somewhere around that time—I used to help with security at the Olympic Auditorium in Los Angeles, which was a popular place to see boxing, wrestling, roller derby, and other events. My mother, Aileen Eaton, was the boss there for 38 years, and she promoted a lot of championship fights. A lot of movie stars like Bob Hope used to come to the Olympic, and even famous criminals like Mickey Cohen. Mickey liked me, and that was a good thing because I didn't realize at the time that he would shoot people he didn't like!

Mauler's Note: This is the same Mickey Cohen who was portrayed by Sean Penn in the movie "Gangster Squad", and he was one bad mamma-jamma.

One night Mickey said, "C'mon Gene, I'll buy you a hot dog." So me, Mickey, and his two gunsels went to the hot dog stand. Mickey's bodyguards weren't very subtle—their jackets would sometimes fall open to reveal big pistols holstered under their arms. Mickey made the hot dog vendor give me two hot dogs on one bun, and he paid the man with a five-dollar bill, which was a lot of money back then. Now, I always got my hot dogs for free because my mother ran the joint, but I never told Mickey that because I didn't want to cost the hot dog guy a big tip. One night, an auditorium employee saw me talking to Mickey and said, "Make sure he doesn't shoot anybody"—as if there was anything I could do about it if he did! (laughs)

Out of all the events at the Olympic, the Thursday night boxing crowds drank the most beer. And that meant more drunk people, which meant more people to throw out. I would always sit in the crowd wearing my street clothes to make everybody think I was just another fan, but the whole time I was keeping my eye on Tom Cornwell, a big cop who my mother had hired for security. Every time Tom took somebody out, I'd get out of my seat and follow them to make sure that none of the troublemaker's buddies were sneaking up behind.

One night, a large, fat gentleman had a little too much to drink and started throwing beer bottles around. So Tom went to get him, and walked him up the aisle to the side door with me following at a distance. But when they got to the door, the guy dug his heels in and refused to move. When Tom put a hand on the guy's shoulder to move him along, the guy spun around and punched Tom in the face—knocked his front teeth right back into his mouth!

Now Tom was the kind of guy who, if he got excited, he wouldn't show it, so he stayed calmer than you would expect. When I ran up to him, he just looked at me and said, "Take this guy into that office right there, I'm going to call a squad car." Then he went to make the call, which left me and the troublemaker alone in a room together.

A couple of minutes later, Tom came back and the guy was laying unconscious on the ground with his front teeth knocked out. Tom kneeled down and looked at the guy, then looked up at me and I said, "I think he drank too much and fainted."

Tom just looked at me for another moment, then he shook his head and smiled. I could tell he wasn't buying my story for a second, but he never said a word as we packed the guy into the cruiser, then went back to work as if nothing had happened at all! (laughs)

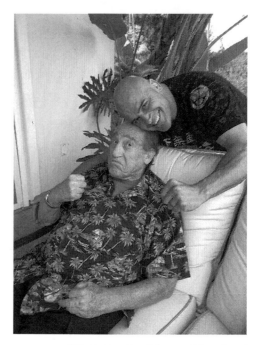

"Uncle Gene" with his good friend and fellow legend "El Guapo" Bas Rutten. Photo courtesy Bas Rutten.

Spying With Larry

My first judo teacher was a guy named Larry Coughran. He wanted to be a lawyer, but while working his way through college, he was also a private detective. He asked me to come along for some of the things he was doing, and he paid me whatever minimum wage was back then to make sure that if anything happened, I'd be there to handle it.

Once, a woman came to Larry and said, "I think that my husband's cheating on me, and he thinks I'm out of town." She gave us her house key, and we went over there when we knew he had some company. The plan was for me to open the door and make sure that nobody got out while Larry took pictures of the people inside.

We snuck up to the door, heard the voices talking, and burst into the room. The husband was in there with his mistress all right, but before Larry could take any pictures, the guy jumped right out of bed, bare-butt naked, and started running for the door! Larry yelled "Grab 'im!" so I had to grab the guy and restrain him. Not only was he bare-ass naked, but he had perfume all over him too. Whether it had rubbed off from her, or he had put it on himself on purpose, I have no idea.

Once I had the guy under control and Larry took his pictures, I let the guy go, and he got back into the bed and pulled the covers over his head. As we were leaving, I turned to Larry and said, "Next time, *I* wanna take the pictures and *you* can hold onto the naked guy!" I mean, I know that the Greeks used to wrestle naked, but even I'm not old enough to have been around for that! (laughs)

Get Gene's autobiography, "The Godfather of Grappling" at:

 *www.amazon.com*

Chapter Ten

THEO ROSSI

Photo courtesy Tracy Lee (CombatLifestyle.com).

"It amazes me that there are people who talk and talk but have never been punched in the face. I find that legitimately fascinating."

Theo Rossi is a Los Angeles-based actor who has appeared in hit TV shows and feature films including *Grey's Anatomy, Lost, Cloverfield* and *NYPD Blue*. But his most famous role by far is that of Juan "Juice" Ortiz in the smash-hit TV series *Sons of Anarchy,* for which he undoubtedly drew a great deal from his upbringing on the mean streets of Staten Island, New York.

Welcome to LA

My father had his first restaurant in Staten Island, and I don't remember a day in my early life where I wasn't working in a restaurant or nightclub in some capacity.

Then I fell into the acting thing, and that led me to LA with five of my friends. We landed—well, I say "landed" when I mean "drove," and it took us eleven days because we partied so much along the way—we landed in LA on Halloween night, 1999. Just six New York guys in a foreign city with $637 between us. It was like, "Okay, we gotta make money," and because we grew up hustlin', we quickly found gigs at various bars scattered around town.

My best friend Mona was, and still is, a six-foot-one, three-hundred-fifty-pound, notorious, famous bouncer from New York. Back home, he was one of the head bouncers at Scores, so when we hit LA, he went right to work at The Roxy, The Whiskey, and all those places. The rest of us got jobs at places like The Saddle Ranch, Mirabel, and The Red Rock.

Occasionally, we'd all work together, like if one guy's place needed extra bodies, that guy would call some or all of the rest of us. We were just hustlin'—waitering, bouncing, hosting, bartending, whatever we could do to make a buck. And it worked. But in the process, our New York way of doing things made us kind of a shock to the LA people.

You see, growing up, we had always fought. I don't remember ever not fighting. That was just what people did—when you got in a disagreement with someone, you had a fight with them. All the time when I was a kid, it was "Meet me by the smokestack after school," and you sorted things out.

When I was fifteen, I got into it with one of my best friends over a girl and we beat the HELL out of each other. Bangin' it out on this beach with a bunch of our friends watching. But the very next day, we were in the pool together at a big Sunday family gathering, and it was all good. Our faces were lumped up like you wouldn't believe, and my mom asked, "Who were you guys fighting with last night?" We both said, "Just some kids," and never admitted that we'd done that to each other because the fight was over and it was settled.

That's just the way it was in New York, you always fought somebody. You didn't tell on them, you didn't run away from them, you fought them. And you lost, and you won, and that was the deal.

But apparently, not in LA.

So this one night, all six of us were working at a bar/restaurant. Mona was hosting and bouncing, I was runnin' around doing whatever. It was kind of a new place so we were all doing whatever was needed.

I was holding a tray as I walked up to a table that had a bunch of Playboy-wannabe kinda girls, and some pretty big guys. I say "big" but I mean "LA big," meaning that they worked out a ton, but you knew they'd never been in a fight. I immediately noticed one dude who had his shirt unbuttoned way too low and was reeking of self-tanner. There is an inordinate amount of jerkoffs in LA, and this guy was so obviously one of 'em, it was ridiculous.

I asked for their drink order, and of course the guy orders a bunch of vodka-Red Bulls. Of course. Because, you know, that's practically the national "I'm a jerkoff" drink. And as I was turning away to put in the order, the guy says, "Hey—do me a favor and hurry up. I'm gonna time you."

I stopped in my tracks and let that sink in for a second, and then I smiled a little and said, "Okay... I get it."

He's like, "You get what?"

And then I SMASHED him in the face with my serving tray.

At first the entire table was in shock. I was obviously expecting his friends to do something, so immediately I'm like, "Let's do this." The guys at the table stood up, but you could see right away that they had no idea how to handle the situation. Mona was the only one of my crew to see what happened, so he came running over and we rushed them out into the parking lot.

We're outnumbered but we're just attacking, we're on the attack. The LA guys started trying to fight back but then this guy Matt, a former marine from Alabama who also worked at that place, he came running out and he's just unloading on people and it's over pretty quick.

The LA guys ran, dragging some of their guys and picking them up, putting them in the car and taking off. And right away our crew had this bond with Matt, this camaraderie between guys who didn't think the LA way, who didn't take shit from nobody. And that's how my crew quickly came to be known around town.

To be honest, that "take no shit from fools" mindset has helped me in the acting business too, because in this business a lot of people say things that aren't true. While there's obviously no punching anymore in the way I deal with jerkoffs, that attitude is translated in a verbal way. I think that when you grow up the way that I did, you don't have the capacity to suffer fools lightly because those people just weren't tolerated.

St. Paddy's Day

One time in the mid 90s, me and some friends were in Manhattan on St. Paddy's Day, headed to a bar on the upper west side. Some of the guys in our crew were Italian, some guys were Irish, some African-American, and we're all walking to the bar. Obviously there was a lot of drunk people around, and this kid who was one of the drunkest walks up to one of my Italian friends and says, "You're not Irish! What are you doing out on St. Paddy's day?!" Yelling it, right in his face.

I was about fifteen feet behind them, and I couldn't hear much of what was being said, but I could clearly see this kid getting in my friend's face. Now, listen—if you let me see that, you let me see you threaten a guy who I've known since I was eight years old, my immediate reaction is to run up and lay you out. Which is exactly what I did.

The guy hit the ground like a sack of bricks, and his friends— who were just as drunk as him—were like, "What the fuck?!!!" I turned to them and said, "Tell your friend to shut up!" which was kind of unnecessary because the kid was already out cold! (laughs) My friends were all laughing their asses off at this—not because I hurt somebody or because we had any serious malice toward this kid, but because to us, that's the way problems were solved, and our response to it was to laugh.

After the kid came back to consciousness, we checked that he was okay and helped him to his feet. Then I looked at him and said, "Don't talk shit. You can't do that." He was immediately like, "Okay, I'm sorry, I'm sorry," and we ended up doing shots with the kid and his friends at the next bar! For the whole rest of the day, the kid was laughing about the whole thing with this big, swollen face! (laughs)

Barney's Beanery

A few years later, I was in LA at Barney's Beanery with my friend Mike Murray, a tough little Irish kid. Skinny, but tough. I went to the bathroom and I had put a coaster over my beer, which obviously means, "Don't take my barstool." When I came back, there was this really drunk guy sitting in my seat next to Mike, and he was in Mike's face going, "It's my birthday! It's my birthday! Say 'Happy Birthday!'"

Now, I have this thing, had it since I was a kid, where my left leg will start to shake a little when it looks like there's about to be a fight. So of course, it started shaking right then. I walked up and said, "Okay, man—'Happy Birthday.' Now scram, hit the bricks." Three of the guy's friends came over, all of 'em pretty big guys, but they were being fairly cool so I just told 'em to get their buddy out of there. But before anybody could do anything, the guy leans really close to Mike's ear and screams one more time, really loud, "IT'S MY BIRTHDAY!"

And I blasted him right in the face.

He fell off the stool and I jumped on top of him and started hittin' him, and then... it was so weird. His friends, these two-hundred-pound guys, they all started screaming like girls. "No! You're gonna hurt him! Stop it!" Like that. It was so bizarre and confusing to me that I actually stopped, looked at them and said, "What is going on here?"

"You just punched my friend!"

"Right... because he was in my friend's face. I mean... isn't that what we do here? This doesn't happen?"

It was so weird, because to me, that was just the way it was done. And that's when I knew I had to reassess the way people handle things in LA. In New York, I would see even old guys fight in bars, but in LA, they don't fight. Almost NOBODY fights, and if you do punch somebody, they think that you're some kind of animal. It actually amazes me that there are people like that, who talk and talk and talk but have never been punched in the face; who just yell at each other and pray that a bouncer comes. I find that legitimately fascinating.

Genuine Toughness

I'm lucky enough to be a good friend and student of Royce Gracie, and Royce will be the first to tell you that the guys who are yelling and saying they're tough, those are usually the ones who aren't. There are always the people who puff up and tell you what they're gonna do, but to me, the scariest people have always been the ones who don't say a word, the ones who look the most unassuming.

That's what I always found with bouncers, especially on the Manhattan club scene. A lot of these guys, you'd see 'em and they're small, I'm talkin' five-foot-eight and a hundred seventy pounds, and they didn't say a word. And I'd be like, "Okay, that's the toughest guy here." On the other hand, sometimes you'd have these giants who never really fought a lot, but they got away with coasting on their size. I learned really quick that you'd often be better off messing with the six-foot-eight, four-hundred-pound monster than you would be if you messed with the little guy. The people who have it, who are the toughest, they're the ones who will never let you know.

I'm addicted to UFC now, and when I'm hanging around with these [fighters] outside of the Octagon, they couldn't be nicer. They avoid fights at all costs, and yet, they're some of the most deadly people in the world. Same goes for my friends who are Navy SEALs. They're like, incredibly peaceful dudes and yet, c'mon, we all know what they do. Or guys like Emilio [Rivera aka "Marcus Alvarez" on *Sons of Anarchy*], who's one of the most legit tough guys I ever met. Or Danny Trejo. These are guys who you just know are bad dudes, and yet they're the nicest people in the world. Danny's life story is outrageous, just outrageous, and he's the nicest guy because he's been through it.

You look at the other guys on *Sons*—Charlie Hunnam's from Newcastle [England], Tommy Flanagan's from Scotland, Kim Coates is from Saskatoon [Canada]—these are people who grew up fighting. In Newcastle, you fought every day, that's what Charlie did. And in Scotland with Tommy, I mean, come on. So when we're around each other, we vibe really well because we're guys who didn't grow up protected. We're not afraid to live in the real world.

Now, I'm not saying that people should get into street fights. But even if they just go spar, or wrestle, or join a Brazilian jiu-jitsu class or Muay Thai class, I think they need to get hit or to have to fight in some way to understand what it feels like. Then they'd have a whole different attitude towards the way they talk to people.

When people are too sheltered, they feel like there's no consequences to what they do. Mona always says, "Everybody's a tough guy until they get rapped in the beak, and then they're like, 'Wait a minute, I thought we were just yellin' at each other!'" Me, I am not yelling in anyone's face unless I am extremely prepared to be in some kind of physical conflict.

I'll tell you something—I've been in, and seen, and been around more fights than I care to think about, but I wouldn't change it for anything. It made me have the massive amount of manners and respect that I have for everybody. For women, for everybody.

@theorossi

www.TheoRossi.com

Chapter Eleven

PETER DeLUISE

Photo courtesy Peter DeLuise.

"It ended up with the doors blowing open and both of us flying out onto the sidewalk. For me, that was fun."

Peter DeLuise, one of the three sons of legendary comedic actor Dom DeLuise, has worn many hats during his show business career. In addition to being a writer, director, and producer, he has starred in a slew of movies and TV series including *Stargate SG-1, Sanctuary,* and *Seaquest DSV.* However, out of his thirty-plus-year body of work, he is best known for his portrayal of officer Doug Penhall in the late-80s crime drama *21 Jump Street*—a role he reprised in the 2012 cinematic reboot alongside fellow *Jump Street* alumnus Johnny Depp.

In addition to his professional skills, Peter's outgoing nature and gloriously demented sense of humor have made him one of the most beloved directors to work in his adopted hometown of Vancouver. On a personal level, I can say that getting to know Peter is the only thing that has taken some of the sting out of never having gotten to meet his dad. Freaking love this guy.

High School Parties

I was on my high school football team, and me and a few of the other players ended up doing security at other students' private parties. They were kind of like house parties but more organized, where you'd have to pay a certain amount of money to get in, and sometimes there was a flat rate added for booze.

It was this really awkward situation, because everyone from my school would be going to these parties, and all night I was dealing with, "C'mon DeLuise, you know me! Lemme in!" These guys couldn't come up with a measly three dollars' admission and they wanted me to give them a pass, which I couldn't do because I'd have a dozen other people complaining that they didn't get the same thing! So that sucked.

Some of the bands that played at those parties had fans with a very high degree of loyalty. There was a gang presence in my school, but those guys paled in comparison to the groupies who would always get into it over whose band was better than the other guy's band. When things hit the fan, I would always try to reason with them, like, "Look... sure, you can beat the other guy up, but the musical talent of your band is still going to be in question. Correct?" It worked about as well as you'd expect.

When the fights inevitably kicked off, I would foolishly jump in and try to grab people to stop them from hurting each other. Now, any bouncer worth his salt knows that you try to deal with fights from the outside—but not me. Oh, no. I would jump right into the middle and end up fighting for my life. And when it was all over, the other bouncers who had to save my ass would look at me and say, "Why did you DO that?! EVERYBODY knows you don't do that, you IDIOT!" And I'd have to acknowledge that I had committed everybody to the wrong course of action, and feel shame. We never had any kind of a plan about that stuff. It was always horribly organized, and I realized pretty quickly that this was a terrible job and I was awful at it.

Bodyguarding My Dad

Later on, after my brothers and I had gotten tall enough to pass for grown-ups, I fell into being a self-appointed member of my dad's kinda-sorta unofficial security team.

Because people always got excited about meeting my dad, it would sometimes spill over into them becoming overly aggressive. Not in an evil or mean-spirited way, but in a way where they would come into his personal space and start to manhandle him a bit.

People, especially drunk people, would have seen him on their TV every week and they'd forget that they didn't actually know him. They'd become very brazen, hugging him and saying "I love you!" and maybe squeezing or even slapping his cheeks, because he had those wonderful, squeezable cheeks.

It was always people who were well-intentioned. They didn't mean my dad any harm, but you know how it is when somebody gets drunk and they're an inch away from you going, "I love you, man!!!"

and you can feel the moisture from their throat on your face. If there was enough of them, it could get serious because he would actually become helpless and very vulnerable.

What made it worse was that they were encouraged by my dad being too nice a guy to say, "Hey, stop, you're squeezing my cheeks too hard" or whatever. He understood that people approached him out of affection because they thought he was hilarious, and it was just that their sense of personal space was out the window.

I went through similar stuff when *21 Jump Street* was on. It doesn't really happen anymore, but there was a time when I was always stressed out because I couldn't walk down the street without people pointing and yelling, "You're that guy!" But that only happens if your show's on the air, and it's been over twenty years since *Jump Street*'s been on so it's very rare now.

Of course, when it does happen it's always at the exact wrong time—like when I'm sitting at a red light with my finger buried up my nose to the second knuckle. That's when someone in the car beside me will look over and go, "Oh my God! It's that guy!" And then they'll turn to the person in the passenger seat and make a gesture with their finger, like, "And he's pickin' his nose, too!" (sighs) Always, man. Why can't I ever get recognized when I'm being cool and doing something awesome?

Anyway, back to my dad. When things got hairy and people were being aggressive, my brothers and I would form a kind of outward-facing perimeter around him and become very still and expressionless. We'd take on the appearance of a kind of secret service detail, and it seemed to work pretty well, especially if we were at a gala event and all dressed up. We got really good at giving the impression that we were my dad's security team, and that if you got rowdy, we'd have to separate you from him.

Because we had this stoic look and were wearing sunglasses at night or something, drunk people would immediately settle down, like, "Oh, right! Sorry!" They'd suddenly become aware that they were in my dad's space. Sometimes they'd ask, "Are you his bodyguards?" but we'd just look at them with blank expressions and not say anything, which made them even more nervous. We never had to push anyone or grab them—just occasionally laying a hand on somebody's arm was all it took to settle them right down. It was some serious *Dog Whisperer* shit.

Good thing nobody ever got wise to the fact that we were really just a bunch of guys acting like security. If the shit ever really did hit the fan, we would have had no idea what to do other than grab my dad and run away screaming.

Peter adopting his father's CANNONBALL RUN alter-ego of "Captain Chaos". Photo courtesy Matty Granger.

Booker

I don't know if this qualifies, but I played a failed bouncer on the pilot episode of a *Jump Street* spinoff called *Booker* that starred Richard Grieco. That episode showed the Booker character trying all these different forms of employment, including being a bouncer in a scene that we shot at a bar on Granville Street in Vancouver.

My character, Doug Penhall, went to meet Booker at work, and during our conversation, stuff started to go down and people got rowdy. So Penhall and Booker leaped into action, only to have it end up with the doors blowing open, and both of us flying out onto the sidewalk. For me that was fun, because most of the time on *Jump Street* I was a policeman, which meant that I had firearms and back-up. I was never scripted to get my ass kicked the way James Garner always did on *The Rockford Files*, so it was cool to be in a scene where no guns got pulled and I didn't win. To be honest, that would probably be a more realistic scenario if I were ever in an actual fight.

As far as real life is concerned, I'll stick to show business. I like going to work knowing that nobody's going to try to punch me in the face.

@RealPDeLuise

www.PeterDeLuise.com

Chapter Twelve

BIG JOHN McCARTHY

Photo courtesy John McCarthy.

"We've got California street thugs brawling with Brazilian maniacs, I'm holding an out-of-control UFC champion against the wall, and all I can think is, 'How do I get into these situations?'"

No discussion of MMA history would be complete without a detailed mention of Big John McCarthy.

A Brazilian jiu-jitsu black belt and retired LAPD officer who saw front-lines action during the 1992 LA riots, Big John was a pivotal figure during the Ultimate Fighting Championship's early days.

From becoming UFC's first head referee to being the primary author of the Unified Rules of MMA, McCarthy has played as large a role in the sport's development as anyone in the business.

Still appearing worldwide as MMA's top referee and as a ring/cageside commentator with whom it has been my honor to share the broadcast booth, John also operates Big John McCarthy's Ultimate Training Academy in Valencia, CA, and educates prospective referees and judges via his universally-respected C.O.M.M.A.N.D. courses.

Cowboy Boogie

When I was twenty-one years old, I worked at a place called Cowboy Boogie. Yeah, that was actually its name. This was in the early 80s, after John Travolta's movie *Urban Cowboy* became a big thing, and guys were dressing up and walking around like they were cowboys. Cowboy Boogie even had a stupid mechanical bull and everything. I worked there with a guy named Joe, who was a good guy and a tough motherfucker, but also a guy who people would try to pick on because he was the smallest out of all the bouncers.

One night at around one in the morning, the manager was having trouble with this guy who kept putting money on one of the pool tables even though "last game" had been called. Finally, Joe went over to tell him to call it a night, and without warning the guy just CRACKED Joe over the head with his pool cue!

Of course, me and the other bouncers jumped in, and the guy's friend also stepped up, so it became the two of them with pool cues against all of us with nothing in our hands. All of us except me, that is. (laughs)

I had this sap that I kept in my pocket, and I pulled it out and hit the instigator right across the face with it. And dude, it was BEAUTI-

FUL! Tore his nose, ripped a gash from his nostril right up to about the midpoint of his eye. Just tore the whole fuckin' thing. He went down to the ground and I stomped him a couple of times, by which point his buddy was pretty much restrained by the other bouncers.

I picked my guy back up to take him outside, and when I took a look at him—WHOA. You know when you do something, and then you go, "Hmmm, I might have gone too far"? Yeah, it was one of those times. So I handed the guy off to another bouncer and quietly slipped behind the bar to stash the sap, because no way did I want to be carrying it when the police showed up.

When the other bouncers got a look at what a mess the guy's face was, they all started asking me, "Man, what did you hit him with?!"

"Hit him with my hand."

"Dude, look at him! Did you have fuckin' rings on or something?"

"Nope. Just hit him with my hand."

Then the police arrived.

"This guy obviously got hit with a bottle."

"Uh-uh. Hit him with my hand."

"No WAY. If you hit this guy with your hand, then you punch like George Foreman!"

"Well, I don't think that I punch like George Foreman, but I swear I only hit him with my hand."

And so it went for several minutes, with me sticking to my story and thinking, "Please don't let them find the sap! Please don't let them find the sap!" (laughs) At least none of the other bouncers had noticed me using it, and I was smart enough to not tell them I had, so there was no risk of anyone letting it slip.

Lucky for me, the police ended up having to accept my story because the sap never got found. With the state of that guy's face, things would not have gone well for me if it had!

Fantasia

Here's a story that shows how stupid I am.

This happened around 1989 when I was already in the LAPD, but also bouncing on the side in a big dance club called Fantasia. I didn't have a work permit so it was illegal for me to do that, but I needed to make money so I did it anyway.

Fantasia's manager was a guy named Rich, and he had me there as more of a negotiator than a hands-on kind of guy. That suited me fine, because by then I had put in a few years in the nightclub security business, and I was at the point where I just wanted to be a "cooler" who dealt with stuff without getting into fights.

One night, Rich came out to where I was standing at the front entrance and said that there was a guy inside handing out flyers for another club. I went inside and quickly spotted a Persian guy trying to hide a handful of flyers from me, so I walked over and told him that he couldn't do that in here.

Now, the guy had been drinking a little bit and he also had a friend with him, so he began to get a little bit mouthy. "You can't tell me what to do," stuff like that. So I told him, "Lookit—you've got about two seconds to get your butt out the door and take your flyers with you," at which point the idiot reached out and grabbed a hold of my sweater. That was a mistake. (laughs)

As soon as he grabbed me, I threw a BIG right hand over the top and just fuckin' decked him. Put him completely out. But then I looked down and saw that I'd cut him badly, both above and below his eye, and I was like, "GodDAMMIT!"

So I picked the guy up, and dragged him up a short flight of stairs to the manager's office, where I dumped him on a couch and called the LAPD. After a few minutes, he woke up a little and started complaining, but I wasn't too worried because I knew the law. As soon as he grabbed me it became a case of battery, and that made my punch an act of self-defense. But while I wasn't concerned about charges, I did start getting kind of bored while waiting for the cops to arrive. And here's where the stupid part comes in. (laughs)

I noticed a garage door clicker sitting on Rich's desk and I thought, "Why would Rich have a garage door clicker in a dance club? That's ridiculous!" Then my wife, who also worked in the club helping to handle the money, came in to check on me because she'd heard that I got into a fight. After reassuring her that it was no big deal, I held up the clicker and said, "Why the hell would Rich have a garage door clicker in here?" She told me to leave it alone, but I kept playing around with it, clicking the thing at her and saying, "Beam me up, Scotty!"

Five minutes went by, and suddenly I heard what sounded like helicopter blades overhead. It got loud enough that I got curious, so I had another bouncer watch the Persian guy while I went outside. I looked up and saw a chopper up above, and then noticed all these LAPD cars parked at a distance. Of course, I figured they had come for the Persian dude, although it did seem like overkill for for just one guy. But whatever. I waved at them to come and get the guy, but they didn't come in. So I kept waving, but still they kept their distance.

What I was about to find out was that the remote I'd been playing with wasn't a garage door clicker at all—it was a 211 silent robbery alarm with a direct link to the LAPD! (laughs) There I was waving and waving, getting more and more frustrated that the police weren't coming in, and it wasn't until the chopper hit me with a spotlight that I realized that maybe it wasn't such a good idea to play "Beam me up, Scotty!" (laughs)

Needless to say, I drew a whole lot of attention that I sure as hell didn't want, and ended up with enforced days off from the LAPD. All because of one stupid asshole who wouldn't stop handing out his flyers in the club!

UFC Mayhem

A few years later, I was refereeing and doing a bunch of behind-the-scenes work for the Ultimate Fighting Championship. I wore a lot of hats in that company, and one of my least favorite duties was keeping people from killing each other at the after-parties. It was not an officially-appointed thing—and believe me, I didn't ask for the job—but I ended up doing it because somehow it was always me who was right in the middle whenever things got out of control.

One of the most memorable incidents happened after UFC 13. I'm pretty sure it was 13 because Mark Coleman was the champion at the time. The show was over, and I was hanging out and trying to relax when I noticed Wallid Ismail [a notoriously crazy jiu-jitsu fighter] getting into a confrontation with Tank Abbott. They were yelling right in each other's faces, getting more and more heated, and as usual I was only a few steps away, thinking, "Here we go again!" (laughs)

All of a sudden, Wallid hauled off and CRACKED Tank in the face, knocking him right on his ass! So of course all of Tank's boys jumped up, and all the Brazilians jumped up, and we were set for a full-scale gang fight. As if that wasn't bad enough, a drunk-off-his-ass Mark Coleman decided to rampage over there like an out-of-control gorilla and start dropping two-handed Mongolian forearm shivers on everybody! I ran over there, picked Mark up from behind, and carried him away while he kept reaching back and trying to hit me, bellowing, "LET ME GO!!! LET ME GO!!!" in that booming voice of his.

Now, I had rolled with Coleman a few times before, and I'll tell you right now that he was the STRONGEST motherfucker I ever trained with. Just a FREAK. So of course that was a matter of concern, as was the fact that I had just made some changes to the UFC rules that probably hadn't put me in Mark's good books.

You see, shortly beforehand, [then-UFC owner] Bob Meyrowitz had asked me to change the UFC rulebook to make the sport less brutal and more TV-friendly. In response, I had taken out things you wouldn't find in other combat sports, like small-joint manipulation, pressure points, groin attacks, and head butts. Now, removing the head butts wasn't an easy decision, because I knew that in doing so, I was RUINING Mark Coleman. One of his favorite techniques was using that big, melon head of his to bash fighters in the face, and I was gonna be the guy who took that weapon away from him. Even as I did it, I couldn't help but think, "Man, this guy's gonna fuckin' HATE me!" (laughs) And so that was front-and-center in my mind as I tried to figure out what to do with this monster while he went crazy trying to escape my grip.

I pushed Coleman belly-first into the wall and yelled in his ear, "Mark, it's John, you gotta stop! You can't do this, you're the champ, you're gonna get in trouble!" But he just kept fighting me and yelling, "LET ME GO, I'M GONNA KILL 'EM!!! I'LL FUCKIN' KILL 'EM!!!"

So now we've got California street thugs brawling with Brazilian maniacs, I'm holding an out-of-control UFC heavyweight champion against the wall, and all I can think is, "How do I get into these situations?" (laughs)

Thankfully, I managed to get Coleman calmed down enough that I could let him go, and the brawl petered out before anyone got sent to the hospital. I'll tell you right now—dealing with a bar full of wannabe tough guys is bad, but dealing with an out-of-control room full of the toughest fighters in the world is something straight out of a nightmare!

For MORE Big John stories, find his autobiography "Let's Get It On" at:

a. *www.amazon.com*

🐦 *@JohnMcCarthyMMA*

🌐 *www.BJMUTA.com*

🌐 *www.MMAreferee.com*

Chapter Thirteen

CHRIS 'MJOLNIR' FRANCO

All photos courtesy Masi Bardi (MasiPhotography.com).

> **"We shambled in, grabbed a table, and I sat there shirtless and covered in blood as I chowed down on calamari and garlic bread."**

A true pioneer of Canadian mixed martial arts, Chris Franco founded his country's first MMA school in 1997, which he still operates today as the FKP MMA academy.

After spending more than two decades racking up victories around the world in MMA, kickboxing, submission grappling and bare-knuckle karate, Franco now oversees one of British Columbia's most successful fight teams.

In addition to training and coaching, Chris also works as a movie and TV stuntman with career credits including *Rumble in the Bronx*, *I Robot* and the Steve Austin/Danny Trejo movie *Recoil*. He is also an ABC-certified MMA judge who has lent his cageside services to SuperBrawl, bodogFIGHT and the Ultimate Fighting Championship.

But before attaining his current status, "Mjolnir" paid the bills via much less-regulated forms of fighting.

The Purple Onion

In the late 90s, I worked at The Purple Onion in Vancouver's Gastown district. It was a wicked place, up on the second floor with a little jazz lounge to one side of the main nightclub. I loved the fresh, raw oysters and the little panini things they used to sell there—I'd sneak into the kitchen, and the chef would sometimes give me a couple for free. Great place—but a hotbed for bullshit.

One night, I'm standing at my post when two guys get into it, and almost instantly one guy's buddies jump in. Now it's a four-on-one cluster of mayhem. The four guys are all on top of the one, pinning him down, but they're also punching each other by accident in their eagerness to get at the guy at the bottom! (laughs)

At that point, I see a friend of the guy who's getting pummeled moving in with a bottle in his hand. Now granted, I'd probably do the same thing if it was my friend getting attacked, but since it's my job to control the situation, I step in front of the guy and say, "DON'T." He stops, so I turn and start peeling one of the attackers off of the pile, but a second later, I hear a bottle smash and I think, "SHIT, the guy just bottled somebody!" But I'm wrong—it's even worse than that.

I turn toward the guy and see that he has broken his bottle on a table, and now he's stabbing it straight at my guts! What happened in the next split-second taught me a TON about how proper training can make the difference between life and death.

A few years earlier, I had trained with a guy named James Keating, who ran a group called Comtech. Comtech was all about edged weapons and small firearms, and Keating was bad news with both—fighting him on the street would have been like hugging a garbage bag full of razor blades. I've never really been into guns, but I always loved Keating's knife disarms, so I did a few seminars with him and religiously drilled what he showed me. Once a week, every week, I practiced—and now all that training was about to come into play.

Without even thinking, I parried the broken bottle and trapped the attacker's arm between my right arm and my side, putting the fingers of my left hand under his nose, and pressing up on that little piece of cartilage between the nostrils to crank his head back and take him over onto his back. Then I sandwiched his right arm between my knees and cranked until I felt the elbow snap. It was all so reflexive that it was almost like I was on autopilot, and it took a couple of seconds for me to realize what I'd done.

By that time, other doormen had shown up and were dealing with the four-on-one. I was eerily calm, I don't know why, but I swear my pulse rate wasn't even above normal. When I picked up the guy who tried to stab me, he was pale-faced and docile as a lamb—obviously in shock. I said, "Your arm is broken, isn't it?" and he mumbled, "Yeah." Then I noticed a broken gold necklace on the ground, which I figured had come off the guy during the scuffle, so I picked it up and put it in his shirt pocket before taking him downstairs and putting him in a cab. The guy actually thanked me before the cab pulled away for the hospital.

As I turned to go back inside, another doorman who saw the whole thing said, "Dude, why were you so nice to him? That guy tried to fucking stab you!" And at that moment, whatever "zen bubble" I was in popped and I went, "SHIT! What did I just do?! I should have broken the other arm as well, and kept the damn necklace!" (laughs)

Franco with students Jethro dela Cruz (right) and Joshua Lam.

The Penthouse

A few years later, I had a rare weekend night off and decided to spend it at The Penthouse, an iconic place in downtown Vancouver. It had, and still has, an old-style marquee out front like you'd see on a movie theater, with a staircase in the lobby that leads up to the main room. The place has some serious history—even Sinatra and the Rat Pack used to drink there.

Mauler's Note: The full history of The Penthouse, which reads like a Hollywood movie, can be found in Aaron Chapman's book "Liquor, Lust and the Law."

That night, I was hanging out with three buddies—a guy named Mark who was a big dude, about two hundred and sixty pounds, former Greco-Roman wrestler and football player, and two other guys named Jason and Leslie who were just average dudes, not especially tough guys or anything.

The place was packed, including a big group of bikers and hangers-on near the bar. Those guys kind of owned their area, and I remember one guy in particular, a big alpha-male type, lurking around with a sleeveless shirt and tattoos going down both arms. He looked to be close to three hundred pounds, and he was strutting around, drinking, being loud, with the other guys following along. But me and my friends just ignored him and stayed on our side of the bar.

Eventually, I left to give a friend a ride home, and it was 2 AM by the time I got back to the club. I really didn't feel like going back up, and had just decided to wait for my friends at the front door when all of a sudden I heard this commotion upstairs. People screaming and swearing, bottles smashing, stuff like that. So I ran up the stairs and looked to my left where the pool tables were, and saw a bunch of guys laying the boots to two dudes on the ground.

I remember thinking, "Oh man, I feel sorry for those guys"— right before I noticed that "those guys" were my buddies, Jason and Leslie! Mark was trying to pull the bikers away, and they were punching him in the head left, right and center. But he was a tough bastard, and he just shrugged off all the punches.

Back then, during violent incidents, I'd sometimes have these weird moments where I'd just click into another mode and act on instinct. This was definitely one of those times because I snapped, actually started growling, and jumped up onto this high table like a silverback or something! (laughs) To be honest, I don't know how that table even fit me because it wasn't very big, and let's face it, I am. (laughs)

I jumped off again, pulled my shirt off, and threw it on the ground. Yeah, I know that's corny (laughs), but I wasn't really thinking at that point. My little display did manage to get the bikers to back off a few feet though, so now the pool table was between the bikers and my friends. That pool table was covered with bottles and glasses, and I double hammer-fisted the table and screamed, "THESE ARE MY FRIENDS, YOU MOTHERFUCKERS!!!" then swept everything off the table so it smashed and shattered on the floor.

At that point, a guy named Caine "Meat Grinder" Munoz walked up to me. Caine was a big, muscular, well-known street fighter who did certain things for certain people, and he had a reputation that made even some of the most powerful gangsters in the city treat him with caution. He and I hadn't crossed paths in any significant way, but we each knew who the other guy was.

The first thing Caine said was really kind of cool—he said, "I saw what happened, but only fight if you want to fight. Don't do it just to entertain these fucking assholes watching. They'll use you if you let them, but you don't owe them shit." I assured him that I wanted to fight, so he said, "I can't get involved because I know these guys and I know you, so I gotta stay neutral. But I will make sure that nobody jumps you from behind, so just let me know who you want." Without even thinking, I pointed at the guys who'd been doing the stomping and said, "Those five guys!" That got a funny look from Caine, because I guess he'd been expecting me to point out just one! (laughs) But he assured me that nobody else would be allowed to jump in.

This was not a smart thing I was doing, but like I said, I wasn't thinking straight. At least I had Caine watching my back, and Mark stepping up to even the odds a little. At that point, one of the biker crew did something very stupid—he decided he was going to be the diplomat. He got right in my face and said, "Back off, Frank!"—the idiot didn't even know my real name—"This isn't about you, Frank! Your friends started it!" I just looked at him and said, "YOU did this?" and then he realized the mistake he'd just made. He said, "No, wait...!" and then BANG, I knocked him out with a left hook.

He barely had time to fall onto the pool table before Mark's big, hairy arms came out of nowhere and yanked the guy out of sight. It happened so quick, it was like something out of a horror movie! Every time I watch Sin City and see Mickey Rourke holding his hands up and saying "MITTS," I think of Mark's meat-hooks ripping that guy away.

I circled around the table and nailed the next guy with a right hook, and as he was dropping, a group of young hockey players who trained at my school joined the fray. After that it was chaos, guys fighting all over the place, and amidst all the battling bodies I sighted on Alpha Male because I knew that was who I had to take out.

I figured this guy was gonna be a challenge, but when he saw me carving through the crowd, he tried to jump over the bar and get away! That actually disgusted me, how he had been a peacock showing his feathers to everybody, but was now running away as soon as somebody stamped their foot. Fuck that, he wasn't gonna get away.

As he tried to climb over the bar, I hit him in the ribs with a left hook/right hook combination, causing a loud grunt of pain before he finally decided to fight. He slid off the bar and lunged forward, trying to grab me in a body lock. But I just barraged him as he came in—uppercuts, hooks, knees to the head—and he dropped to the ground and tried to turtle up. As he lay there, I unloaded another barrage to make a statement to all his cronies, and I eventually knocked the guy out completely.

I got up to see who else needed to be dealt with, and then I heard one of my hockey player students screaming. A biker had one of the kid's fingers in his mouth, and he bit the thing clean off! After the fight, that bite wound would get so infected that it kept him in the hospital for a week, and even though we found the finger, they couldn't reattach it. But that kid ended up being a real soldier, calling it "the ultimate war wound" and saying that the stump gave him a story that he could tell for the rest of his life.

But back to the fight, which by now had spread out so much that the cops who were arriving couldn't handle it. They just barricaded off a big section of the street outside, and started pepper-spraying people as they ran out the door! It was havoc—girls were trying to get out of there but almost everybody was getting sprayed as they tried to get away. I was still going berserk inside the club, driving the bikers toward the staircase and unknowingly sending them straight into the arms of the spray-happy cops.

Finally, Caine grabbed me by the arm and snuck me and my friends out the door while the cops were occupied with other people. A guy I knew named Nav Chima actually lifted Jason, who was having trouble walking, and carried him out of there for us. I never forgot that, I really appreciated it.

Once we got past the cops, we made our way down the street and past the barricades to where Caine's big red SUV was parked. And then, as we were waiting for Caine to unlock the doors, I saw one of the bikers who had been stomping Jason and Leslie! He was one of the only guys I'd gotten a really strong visual on, so I recognized him clear as day. I guess he recognized me too, because he was trying to avoid eye contact and act like he had nothing to do with anything.

By now, I was a mess. My hands were swollen to twice their normal size, my lips were busted, I was covered in bruises and scratches and blood, but at that moment I didn't give a shit. I pointed at the guy and said, "GET OVER HERE!" and he actually did. He walked over to me and said, "What?" and I said, "You know what!" and neck-clinched him, pulling his face into the crown of my head for a series of rapid-fire head butts. His nose EXPLODED and he dropped like a sack of potatoes.

That used up the last of my adrenaline, and I needed to get the hell out of there. So Caine loaded us into his SUV and took us to a restaurant called Crantini's, which on weekends became a really shady after-hours. We shambled in, grabbed a table, and I sat there shirtless and covered in blood as I chowed down on calamari and garlic bread! (laughs)

My hands were so swollen and sore that I could barely hold a fork, and when Caine noticed that, he got the idea that he would pull on my fingers to straighten them and relieve the tension. But Caine was actually quite intoxicated, and probably not the best guy to be performing battlefield medicine. (laughs) He started pulling my fingers HARD, just yanking on them and saying, "This is good for you! Let me do it!" and I'm like, "AAAAH! Leave my fingers alone! No!" (laughs) We were having this ongoing battle until Crantini's owner, this really nice guy named Mario, came over and said, "Look, I love you guys, but you're scaring everybody in the place. Can you please just put a shirt on and eat your food?" (laughs)

I've grown out of all that ridiculousness now, so much so that it almost feels like it happened to somebody else. Today, I've got a wife and a daughter and a successful business, and fighting in bars is the last thing I want for myself or any of my students.

But having said that, I still have to admit that although that crazy fight resulted in sore, sleepless nights for a week after, thinking about it still puts a little smile on my face.

 @FKPMMA

www.FKPMMA.com

Chapter Fourteen

LANCE STORM

Photo courtesy Lance Evers.

"Jericho came running out and said, 'If any of the boys get in trouble, I saw the whole thing, but if not, I was never here!'"

In the summer of 1991, I traveled over 2000 miles to train in Calgary, Alberta at the Hart Brothers Pro Wrestling Camp. And the first wrestler I met there was twenty-two-year-old chief instructor Lance Evers, aka Lance Storm.

Over the following two decades, Storm would become one of the best friends I've ever had, as well as one of the most universally-respected and criminally-underutilized talents to work in the "Big Three" of WWE, WCW and ECW.

Now living in semi-retirement in his adopted hometown of Calgary, Lance still accepts sporadic bookings around the world when he's not instructing students at the globally-acclaimed Storm Wrestling Academy.

Malarkey's

It was the early winter of 1991, and [Chris] Jericho and I were working at Malarkey's, a dive bar attached to a Calgary hotel. On the night in question, we had just returned from our first tour of Japan, and I believe it was our first shift since getting back. Working with us were a new guy named Scotty and a guy named Big Tony, who was a student of mine at Hart Brothers. Tony was also... how shall I put this... a big, jacked up, "supplemented" fellow with a mustache, crazy hair, and anger management difficulties.

Tommy, our manager, was off for the night and the hotel manager, a skinny guy named Bill, was pulling double-duty. It was a very uneventful night, and after we wrapped things up, Jericho and I got into his beat-up '76 Volare and began pulling out of the parking lot.

As we cruised past the glass doors of the hotel lobby, I spotted some guy beating the hell out of someone in there, so I yelled at Jericho to hit the brakes. After he did, I jumped out and ran into the hotel, and as I pulled open the doors, I realized that it was Bill who was getting beaten up. So I grabbed Bill's attacker and threw him through the open door to Jericho, who grabbed the guy as he was stumbling and threw him further out into a concrete divider that had some shrubs or hedges on it that the cold weather had reduced to a bunch of bare twigs. Jericho threw the guy hard enough that he got buried in the mass of bristles, after which we turned back to check on Bill.

As we were helping Bill up, we suddenly saw Tony charging across the parking lot like a raging bull. He pulled Bill's attacker out of the bushes, threw him hard to the ground, then picked him up and chucked him back into the bushes. Tony was in full rage mode, just rag-dolling this guy as he repeatedly chucked him to the ground, then into the bushes, then back to the ground again.

At the time, Jericho was helping me to teach the classes at Hart Brothers, and he had developed a very short tolerance for Tony and his stupidity. So he ran outside, gave Tony a kind of a tackling shove and said "Tony, that's enough, you're going to kill him!"

Without missing a beat, Tony's eyes fixed on Jericho as his new focus of rage, and you could tell that he was about to take a swing. But although Jericho's not the biggest dude—and he'll tell you himself that he's not a trained fighter—he will not back down from anyone. He once stood up to Bruiser Bedlam, a giant power-lifter who could have squashed Jericho under his thumb, and in later years [Jericho] would fight Bill Goldberg to a stalemate in a WWE locker room.

Seeing what was about to happen, Jericho decided to launch a pre-emptive strike. Now, bear in mind that he was wearing tight jeans and cowboy boots [while standing] on icy pavement—with the jeans tucked into the boots because that was apparently way cooler—so he did not have the best attire for grip and mobility. But he didn't care, and he launched himself at Tony with what would have been a perfect cross-body block if he had been in a wrestling ring. But sadly for him, he wasn't.

Tony either ducked with perfect timing or just conveniently slipped—either way, he dropped at just the right moment to send Jericho sailing clear over his head. The landing was not pretty, with Jericho hitting the ground and skidding several feet along the ice.

At that point, Scotty was just leaving the bar, and he ran over to me and said "I'll get Chris, you get Tony!" I was like, "Oh great—I get the two-hundred-forty-five-pound raging fool." But I guess Scotty figured that since I was dating Tony's sister at the time, Tony would be inclined to like me a little better and maybe not try to kill me.

I somehow managed to hook Tony [lock him up with a submission hold] and pin him to the ground long enough to calm him down. Scotty had an easier time than me, since Jericho was only mad at Tony and not inclined to take his anger out on anyone else. So once we finally got Tony settled down, I let him up and sent the big galoot on his way.

I don't recall what happened to the guy who started the whole thing. I guess he either ran away during the melee or he's still laying in that pile of twigs to this day.

Hairbag Thursday

Malarkey's owners eventually decided to gut the place and re-open under a new name, so this next incident happened on the final weekend of the club's existence as we knew it.

Thursday was always the big night for the club—I used to call it "Hairbag Thursday." They'd play classic rock, and all these guys with baseball caps and long hair and dirty jeans would come in, and it was by far the biggest night of every week.

The hairbags were nothing if not entertaining. For example, one night at the DJ booth, a rather inebriated First Nations fellow requested—slurringly—that the DJ play the "Slow Motion Walter" song. This confused us so we inquired further, to which he replied, "Walter, he's the fire engine guy." That didn't help much, so he started to sing it to us:

"Slooooow Motion Waaaalter... the FI-yer EN-jin guy..."

Yes, he thought, "Smoke on the water, and fire in the sky" by Deep Purple was about a slow moving fireman named Walter! We laughed so hard, I still sing those lyrics when I hear this song.

Anyway, during last call on the final Thursday, a group of regulars who Tommy the manager had always been particularly lenient with asked if they could dance on the bar. Since this was the club's last hurrah weekend, Tommy said yes, which could have been a really bad idea. But we got lucky and nothing disastrous happened.

The next night, a hairbag came in who hadn't been there the night before. I guess he'd heard about the other hairbags getting to dance on the bar, and he was upset that he missed it. So he asked Tommy if he could do it, and once again, Tommy said yes.

Just as this was happening, I got a call from the hotel saying that there was a problem in the lobby. I went through the adjoining door and saw the lady manager of the hotel pointing outside, where a guy was beating the hell out of a cabbie. I recognized the guy from having thrown him out of the bar maybe an hour before, and I got out there and pulled him away. The cabbie was more or less okay, but he wanted to press charges, so the manager asked me to restrain the assailant while she called the cops. I did, but got bored while waiting and figured that I may as well put my time to good use. So I started practicing my hooks [submission holds], switching around from front chancery, to cross-face chicken wing, to double arm bar, and so forth.

After a couple of minutes of that, the back door of the bar opened and out rushed an off-duty Jericho, still wearing his jeans tucked into his beloved cowboy boots. He said, "You have to get back in there, all hell's broken loose! If any of the boys get in trouble, I saw the whole thing—but if not, I was never here!" (laughs) It sounded more important than an idiot who punched a cabbie, so I let the guy go and ran back into the bar.

All the lights in the place were now on, the room was filled with dust and smoke, and the ceiling above the bar had caved in. On the dance floor, it was chaos with people screaming and yelling, the bouncers trying to break up fights, people bleeding, and I was like, "What the hell happened?"

It turned out that the idiot hairbag who wanted to dance on the bar had decided it would be a good idea to do chin-ups on a fake wood beam structure that was attached to the ceiling. He couldn't pull himself up, but being a particularly hefty hairbag with a fat ass and a big belly, he unfortunately managed to pull the whole ceiling down.

A couple had been standing close to the bar when it happened, and the girl got clipped by a piece of beam. The boyfriend immediately became enraged, and threw his beer bottle at the guy he thought was responsible. But of course, he threw his bottle at the wrong person, and it shattered against the wall next to a guy who had absolutely nothing to do with it. The innocent bystander got sprayed in the face with broken glass, and ended up losing the vision in one eye. I later found out that the guy who threw the bottle was violating his parole by even being in a bar, and he ended up going back to jail.

We were all stuck giving witness statements and filling out police reports until five in the morning, and as the sun came up, I shambled away thinking that this was obviously the last night for Malarkey's. But to my surprise, by the next night they had managed to get most of the debris dragged out of there for one final night of partying in the wreckage.

If you ask anyone who worked there, though, they consider "The Night The Roof Caved In" to be the final night of what was undoubtedly the scuzziest bar I ever worked in.

For MORE Storm Stories, check out "Storm Front" and "Storm Warning" at:

a *www.amazon.com*

🐦 *@LanceStorm*

🅦 *www.StormWrestling.com*

Chapter Fifteen

HAILEY BOYLE

Photo courtesy Hailey Boyle.

"I'd never seen angry like this before—his face was turning purple and he was punching the steering wheel. That's when I realized I was being kidnapped."

Standing six-foot-two, Hailey Boyle is both the runt of the litter in a gigantic family, and possibly the largest female comedian on the planet.

A cousin of outlandishly-eccentric MMA fighter Matt Horwich, Boyle spends much of her time performing in far-flung locations including Europe, Greenland, The Bahamas, and Central America.

But before making her living behind a microphone, Boyle stocked her arsenal of jokes and bizarre stories by working as the only lady bouncer in the no-rules town of Fairbanks, Alaska.

The Marlin

I worked at a club called The Marlin in Fairbanks. It was a pretty dumpy-looking place, half-underground in a brown wood building with a hostel and pawnshop above it. It had a fenced-in section out back where everybody went to smoke weed, and a giant sailfish over the entrance. Yeah, I know that a sailfish is not the same thing as a marlin, but nobody seemed to care.

From the outside, the place looked like nothing, but on the inside, it was all kind of weird and cool. They had a wood stove, and strange carpets where if you spilled something, the carpet wouldn't even be wet—whatever you spilled was just gone. To this day, I still wonder what's under there.

I was lucky to get a job there because EVERYBODY wanted to work at The Marlin. It was pretty much the only place to go in town, so it was packed every weekend. And not just for the regular reason that bars get packed—it was also full all the time because people went there to poop.

You see, Fairbanks is WAY the hell north, and a lot of people live in cabins with no running water. Often, university students or other out-of-towners who were unused to the lifestyle would not be cool with making in an outhouse—especially when it's cold enough to kill you—so they'd save it until they came to The Marlin. But the water pressure in the toilets was weak, and they were always getting clogged so it was a constant nightmare.

The Marlin didn't have a coat check. You don't see a lot of coat checks in Alaska because the sheer volume of coats would be overwhelming. But as a courtesy, and to pass the time, I sometimes ran an informal coat check on the bench next to the front door. I would make good money in tips doing that and collecting the cover, because in Fairbanks, no matter what you do, if you have boobs, you're getting tips.

Live music was, and still is, the coolest thing about The Marlin. One night we had a band booked, and a friend of mine gave me a bunch of acid to sell for $5 a hit. So all night I checked ID's, took the cover, and dosed the crowd. A few hours later, I had sold every last hit of acid, and everybody in the bar was absolutely tripping balls—me and the band included! I was actually very proud of myself, because I found out that I could trip really, really hard and still do my job effectively.

Crazy Dreadlocks Guy

Once in a while we'd get this big, hulking guy in the bar who was part of a crew of angry-hippie types—white people with dreadlocks and facial tattoos who all lived in a cabin together, and had a black school bus with a purple coffin on its roof. It was painted all over with slogans like "Life is a prison that you're sentenced to for the crime of being born." Nice, right?

Every time this guy came in, he would be WASTED and out of control after only one beer. I don't know what his deal was, but he was like, the ONLY guy in Alaska without any alcohol tolerance. He was also at least six-foot-four which made him a handful, but I grew up with giant brothers who didn't like me, so I could deal. My usual trick with customers was to make them think we were leaving together, and then ditch them outside. Another method that I started using in high school was to shove guys against the wall, and hold them there till they calmed down. I'm really good at it, and if they're small, I can even lift them up so their little feet dangle. But since this guy was too big to shove and too sloppy to flirt with, I had to use a different strategy.

With him, I'd just start a fight, which wouldn't take much doing. Then I'd dodge all his punches while backing up and luring him out the door. He'd keep lunging in my direction, and I'd reach out once in a while to keep him from falling while I stayed out of the way of his fists. It usually worked flawlessly, although one time he did clip me in the face. For a second, I was real mad, but then I thought, "No, don't knock him out, because then you'll have to carry him and he's really big." He never came in one time without getting really violent, and I don't know why they never completely eighty-sixed the guy. I think the owner was scared of him.

Streakers

Another time, a bunch of streakers ran through the bar, which wasn't a big deal because they were all people that we knew. They came running through the front door, went out the back and through the weed-smoking area, and climbed over the fence. Then they circled around and did it a second time, and then came back for a third. But the third time, this pretty girl named Leah stayed behind on the dance floor, completely naked and dancing with everybody.

Even The Marlin's owner was sitting on the bar and watching, and I had to remind him, "Hey Patrick, you know we're in violation of a bunch of health codes, right?" To which he and everybody around me responded, "WHO CARES?!! NAKED GIRL IN THE

BAR!!!" Meanwhile, all the women in the place were either uncomfortable as crap or doing their best to pretend it was no big deal.

Leah was dancing around in this kind of Grateful Dead spinner haze, not responding to anyone. She was gone, lost in her own little world, which made it kind of awkward because I had to find a way to get a hold of her and say, "Get out or put some clothes on" without bumping into her lady parts or something. I could tell that she had just enough awareness to be clearly enjoying me being uncomfortable, but I finally got hold of her shoulders and told her to leave out the back door.

All at once, every guy in the place went "AAAAAAWWWWW!" but I was like, "C'mon guys, she's not even wearing underpants! We can't have snail trails all over everything."

Wanted Ben, Got Dave… And Kidnapped

At one point, I started going out with a guy named Dave [who was] from a nearby village called Bethel. Bethel was the kind of place where they have 200 words for "snow" but zero words for "rape" or "thank you." You know, the kind of place where incest is not a social faux pas, and everyone's ankles and knees are on backwards from inbreeding. But Dave was actually okay—really sensitive but also a rough-and-tumble kind of guy at the same time. He did do two things that drove me nuts, though—he had a neck beard, which I just couldn't tolerate, and he used to wear a sweater with a vest over top of it. You don't do that, you just don't.

I actually had a crush on Dave's best friend Ben, who was a chubby frat boy and a fellow bouncer at the bar. But Ben was engaged and a "Mr. Morality" type, so kind of by default I ended up with

Dave. Wanted Ben, got Dave—everybody knew it. Even Dave knew it. But the men in Alaska are incredibly dedicated and when they like you, they are NOT letting go. With ten men for every woman, they kind of have to take what they can get. They even have a saying: "In Alaska, you don't lose your wife, you just lose your turn."

I ended up breaking up with Dave not once, not twice, but every single day for three months. I constantly reminded him, "We are not a couple, we do not have a future, we are just friends who happen to be having sex." But he would still show up at the bar all the time, and drive me around, and bring food and cigarettes to my house. I even made a rule that if he brought me food, he had to bring some for my roommate Cristina as well. Even though I kept telling him that we weren't together, he'd come over all the time with pancakes, mac 'n cheese, and all the food that he knew I liked.

Every time he came into the bar, he'd take the same spot across the stage from where I was sitting and just stare at me, silently crying like that Indian on the pollution commercial. Occasionally, he'd get up and drift by without making eye contact, saying stuff like, "I know you like Ben more than you like me." And I'd be like, "Yup! Everybody knows that!" It was very, very awkward. I was trying to phase him out, but he was just too handy to have around. Plus, I'm a sucker for a huge dick, and his was GINORMOUS—he is the only man I have ever known who could actually suck his own dick. You would have had trouble saying goodbye too, I promise.

The last straw was when a band called Yukon Rider came through town. A lot of the hippies in town thought that band was hokey, but I loved 'em. Still do, got 'em on my iPod. For some reason, the band's lodgings fell through, and it was up to me to find them places to stay. Since I'd been flirting all night with a member of the band who was kinda cute in a dorky, beardy/glasses kinda way, I decided that he would come home with me.

We didn't have full-on sex but I did make him go down on me, and the next morning, we were laying in bed naked when Dave came walking in with breakfast for me and Cristina. Now, remember that this is Alaska, and I lived in this weird, half-rotten river cabin with no lock on the door, and not even a door on my bedroom. So when Dave marched in, he immediately saw what was going on. Without a word, he just put the food down, turned around and walked out. I turned to the band guy and said, "This ain't gonna be good" and he said, "Yeah, I don't think my fiance's gonna like it either." Um, what? FIANCE?! I had no idea that he had a fiance, so I kicked him out and I did not share my chicken fingers with him.

For the next two days, Dave called me at least once per hour, crying and saying stuff like "Let me know if you need anything—I know we're not gonna be together, but I wanna make sure we'll be friends." After a bunch of these calls, he finally got me while I was getting ready for work and he offered me a ride. I figured, what the hell, I'd let him pick me up, since I did still want to be friends.

He picked me up in his big, ridiculous rear-wheel-drive work truck with a yellow light on top. We headed toward The Marlin, but at one point he turned right when he shouldn't have. I asked him where he was going, and he burst into tears, saying, "I just feel like if I let you out of this car, I'm never gonna see you again!"

All of a sudden, he was swinging back and forth between hysterically crying and being so angry... I'd never seen angry like this before. His face was turning purple, and he was punching the steering wheel so hard that he broke the horn casing. He was running red lights and driving like a maniac in a work truck that had zero traction, and I really started to panic. That's when I realized that I was basically being kidnapped, and I started to cry too because I thought he was going to kill us both. No matter how much I asked him to, he wouldn't stop the car—he just kept driving and saying "I feel like I'm losing you forever."

I eventually got my wits about me and started making promises, "Yes, we're gonna be friends. Yes, we're still gonna see each other. Yes, it's gonna be cool, just stop the car..." After a LOT of that, I finally got him to pull into a laundromat. I immediately jumped out of the truck, walked to work, and told everybody what had just happened.

Now, if this had happened in Manhattan you'd probably call the cops, but in my case nobody bothered because in Fairbanks, the state troopers never came when you called them anyway. The only time you'd see them is when they paid surprise visits to The Marlin trying to bust people for smoking weed. So basically, the whole situation blew over.

The last time I saw Dave was years later after I moved out of Alaska. I had come back for a friend's wedding, and I guess Dave hadn't heard that I was back in town. When he saw me, he accidentally swallowed the rollie cigarette he was smoking, turned purple, bent over, and vomited. Then he looked up and said, "Hey, what's up?" as if he didn't have barf on his shirt. It was awesome.

The Odds Are Good...

Two days after my kidnap experience with Dave, I made out with a guy named Nate in the fenced area out back, and this was a guy I actually liked so we started dating. Not like I did with Dave, we were genuinely dating. And in true Alaska style, he instantly became insanely possessive, and told me that he wanted to get married so

I could stay at home and not work at the bar. Of course I told him "No way," so he started showing up at the bar every night to make sure that no other guy made a move.

One night, I was doing a walk-through and I saw Nate and this old native dude trying to start a fire in the wood-burning stove. That wasn't unusual since we often put customers in charge of starting the fire, but at one point I thought I overheard Nate saying something about using motor oil. Not thinking much of it, I just reminded him about the bar's "no accelerants" rule and kept walking.

The next morning, I got a call from the bar owner's wife, who told me that the bar had burned down. I immediately thought what I still think today—that my boyfriend burned it down so I wouldn't work there anymore. The fire department even said that the fire had started in the vicinity of the stove.

As if that wasn't enough to put me on my guard, three days later Nate dropped by my cabin when I wasn't around, and left me a pair of Smith & Wesson handcuffs and an extendable baton that he had stolen from a cop! I still have them—handcuffs and a handcuff key that might technically be a felony for me to possess. And on the same day, Nate gave a girlfriend of mine the same things! I don't know what the implication was with those gifts, but I sure as hell wasn't going to ask him to show me.

That's why straight women in Alaska have a saying about their dating options: "The odds are good, but the goods are odd."

🐦 *@HaileyButter*

🌐 *www.HaileyBoyle.wix.com/haha*

Chapter Sixteen

DON 'THE PREDATOR' FRYE

Photo courtesy Susumu Nagao.

"One of the customers walks in and points out three bullet holes in the wall, right behind where I'm standing."

In addition to possessing what is undoubtedly the greatest mustache of all time, former Arizona firefighter and two-time UFC tournament champion Don "The Predator" Frye stands as one of the pivotal figures in the evolution of mixed martial arts.

In 1996, after amassing over 700 victories in wrestling, judo and boxing, Frye threw his ten-gallon hat into the UFC Octagon at the

"David vs. Goliath" tournament in Bayamon, Puerto Rico. After knocking out the 410-pound Thomas Ramirez in eight seconds, and defeating all three of his opponents in a total time of 3:10 to win the tournament, Frye went on to build a legendary career filled with all-time classic matches against the likes of Tank Abbott, Ken Shamrock and Yoshihiro Takayama.

But before any of that, he was just a struggling college wrestler making ends meet by teaching wannabe tough guys what the word "predator" really means.

Eskimo Joe's

This happened back around 1989 or so, when I was wrestling on the Oklahoma State team. After practice, me and one of the other [team members] go to this place in Stillwater, Oklahoma called Eskimo Joe's, and we go upstairs and start drinkin'. After a couple hours, we look out the window and see my then-wife and the other guy's girlfriend climbing out of their truck, comin' to pick us up.

So we start walkin' across the bar, and we're passin' a pool table when this guy [who's playing at the table] up and shoves me. Big ol' weightlifter type. Then he starts cussin' at us—I don't remember most of what he said 'cause I was so drunk, but I do remember him sayin' "I wanna kick both your asses!"

I'm just standin' there holding my beer, and my buddy takes my arm and says, "Let's go", but I say, "No, I wanna hear what this guy's got to say." So I put my beer down on the pool table, and then the guy charges straight at me. Now, if you know what you're doin' it's hard to miss a target that big, so—BOOM—I hit 'im, and he drops to his knees. But on the way down, he grabs my shirt and rips it! Brand new, ten-dollar shirt—back then that was a lot of money for a shirt, especially when you're in college.

So now he's in front of me on his knees, and I'm so pissed about the shirt that I hit 'im again, and he goes completely out. Then the bartender comes over and tells me I gotta leave. Hey, I didn't start it! But I was leavin' anyway, so we go downstairs as my wife's walkin' through the door, and she sees my shirt all ripped up and starts yellin' at me, "You got into a fight, didn't you, dammit?"

She's still yellin' when the big guy comes downstairs with all his friends. He's bleedin' from the face like a stuck pig, but he still looks at me and says, "C'mon, you and me, let's go outside!" I was all for it, but my wife turns to him and goes, "Haven't you had enough? Look at you!", and he pretty much cowers down to her. So nothing happens and we all head home.

At this point I'm thinkin' the situation's all blown over. But a week later, I get a call from that same sonofabitch—who somehow got my number—and he wants me to pay for his emergency room visit! He says, "They found glass in my head, you must have hit me with a glass!", and I say, "You're fulla shit. I didn't hit you with a glass, I hit you with my fist. You can kiss my ass!"

An hour later, the damn police call and they want me to come in and make a report. So I go down to the Stillwater police station, and on the way there I'm thinkin' that I gotta make this look good. I figure I'll play up the size difference—I mean, I was a two-hundred-and-five-pound heavyweight, and this guy was a big powerlifter, had to be at least two hundred and eighty pounds.

So the cops ask me, "What happened?" and I say, "This guy started some shit and got hold of something he couldn't handle. But I was just acting in self-defense—after all, I'm just a little guy, I'm only two hundred pounds."

The cop gives me a funny look, and then he goes, "We know who the fuck you are, dummy—you're the heavyweight from the wrestling team!"

So they weren't buyin' it, but they were still happy to let the whole thing slide, and tell the other guy to let it go. A couple of days later, just when I think I've finally heard the last of it, the manager of Eskimo Joe's calls me up and offers me a job! (laughs)

Mama's Boy

A while after that, I'm workin' at the job I got from kickin' that guy's ass, and we got a huge lineup out front. This pretty boy, college boy, comes walking right up to the front and tries to go in. I stop 'im and he goes, "Do you know who my mom is? My mom's on the city council!" I look at the other bouncer and we both bust out laughing. The guy actually did get in, because he slipped past us while we were laughing too hard to chase him down! I mean, can you imagine that? Being twenty-one years old and using your mom's name to get into a bar? You do that, you're going nowhere in life. You're a puss.

La Perla

The next year, I was a bouncer at a place called La Perla in Glendale, Arizona. Only five bucks an hour and I had to drive across town to get to work. One night, I'm at the front door, and one of the waitresses comes out and says that there's a guy inside givin' her trouble.

I go in there and see this Mexican guy, Mexican national, already surrounded by a couple of the other bouncers. I tell him it's time to leave and he walks out on his own, but I'm watchin' him because the whole way to his car, he's fumbling in his pockets like he's lookin' for a knife or something.

After he gets in his car and the other bouncers go inside, he drives up to about fifteen feet away from me, rolls down his window and says, "You know what? I think I'm gonna kill one of you motherfuckers." And then he shows me what he was rootin' around in his pockets for— a goddamned pistol!

Well, I go straight inside, close the door, walk over to the manager and say, "I quit!" He says, "Why?" and I says, "Because that guy said he was gonna kill me." Then the manager goes, "You can't let these guys intimidate you!" and I couldn't believe that. "Intimidate me, hell," I says. "I'm gettin' guns pulled on me for five dollars an hour? I quit!"

Not that the next [job] was any better—bartending at a dive bar in Sierra Vista. Easy gig—you could have beer, or if you wanted a mixed drink, it had to be mixed with water or Coke. That was about as fancy a drink as you was gonna get in that place—you'd only ask for an umbrella in your drink if you wanted to start a fight.

One of the customers walks in one night and gets to talkin', and after a few minutes he points out three bullet holes in the wall right behind where I'm standing. He tells me that a few weeks before, somebody had tried shootin' him and the bullets had left those holes there. Goddamn!

I'll tell ya what, I was a hell of a lot safer in the Octagon with Tank Abbott or Mark Coleman than I was in some of them places I worked at!

🐦 *@DonFryeFighter*

🌐 *www.ThePredatorDonFrye.com*

126

Chapter Seventeen

DIAMOND DALLAS PAGE

Photo courtesy Dallas Page.

"It was the first time I ever got a round of applause for busting a nut!"

During pro wrestling's "Monday Night Wars" boom period, Diamond Dallas Page (aka "DDP") was one of the biggest names in the business. After learning to wrestle at the almost-unprecedented age of 35, Page silenced his many doubters with a career that included three world title reigns in the World Championship Wrestling organization.

After suffering a serious back injury and taking up yoga to repair it, Page modified the standard poses and combined them with other bodyweight exercises to create a system he calls "DDP Yoga." Since its release, DDP Yoga has produced a laundry list of miraculous recovery stories, with high-profile endorsers like WWE legend Chris Jericho pouring out of the woodwork.

But long before he got involved in professional wrestling or yoga, Dallas Page was a bouncer and manager at some of New Jersey's busiest nightclubs.

Jimmy Byrne's

I first started bouncing in the late 70s at a club called Jimmy Byrne's Sea Girt Inn. Man, that place was pumpin'! I was seventeen years old, and at first, my job was just cleanin' up the joint. But even though I was so young, I was already six foot four, so the management thought I was older than I was. So one night when they were short a bouncer, they asked if I wanted to work the door, and of course I said, "Hell, yeah!"

I'd snuck into the club a couple of times before, and I'll tell ya, back then, trying to get laid at seventeen in a club left you feeling like you couldn't get laid with a fistful of pardons in a women's prison! But once I put that shirt on, that Jimmy Byrne's T-shirt, women were comin' up to me left and right who wouldn't be caught dead talkin' to me otherwise! I was like, "What the fuck is happening here?" and that's when I realized that when you work as a bouncer, you got stroke!

Shortly after that, I noticed a hierarchy in the bar that still applies in bars today. To put it in wrestling terms, if you're workin' on the floor, then you're one of the boys on the undercard; if you work the front door, you're a mid-card guy; and if you're a bartender, you're one of the top guys. But if you're the manager—and I don't care what you look like—if you're the manager and you have any kind of charisma at all, then you're the fuckin' main event!

I saw that the manager of Jimmy Byrne's was forty-five or fifty years old, five foot eight, balding, out of shape... but he still had young pussy all over him! And I'm thinkin', "Fuck, I want THAT job!" Because, let's be honest—if you join a band, it's because you want pussy; if you play sports, you wanna be the star to get pussy; and if you work in the bar business, it's DEFINITELY to get pussy! And in the bar business [it's easier because] they're drunk, they got a buzz on! How easy is that? Especially in the late 70s and early 80s before AIDS really hit, and casual sex was a sport!

Nut Bustin'

One incident still stands out in my mind. The bar I was working at at the time would always blow up late on Sunday afternoons. They'd serve fifty-cent drinks and we'd have 1,500 people in the place. One Sunday, right before it was about to pop, I found this chick that I'd been wanting to hit for, like, FOREVER, and I took her into a room where they stored all the beer that wouldn't fit in the cooler. We fucked in there for about twenty minutes while the place filled up, and when we walked out, there was nine guys all lined up, clapping and cheering and yelling "AWESOME!" (laughs) It was the first time I ever got a round of applause for busting a nut!

I probably worked at twelve different clubs up and down the Jersey Shore, and that whole time I was workin' my way up from bouncer, to bouncer/bar back, to the front door, to being a bartender. You can climb the ladder fast if you carry yourself right. Just like my wrestling persona of Diamond Dallas Page was about creating the gimmick and walkin' the talk, in the nightclubs it was all about creating the hype.

Wardrobe Malfunction

We had some wild fights in some of those places, man. Me, I was never a fighter who liked to knock guys out. I preferred to put 'em in front facelocks or whatever hold I needed to use to get 'em out the door. I remember one night, a motorcycle gang rolled in and the shit hit the fan. I ended up tangling with this guy who wasn't even part of the [gang]. I hooked him [put him in a submission hold] and started taking him out. Then one of my buddies came running over while I was still holding the guy, and just punched him in the fuckin' face! We had to wear white pants as part of our uniform, and blood went all over my pants! I was so pissed—who has their bouncers wear white pants, anyway? That's fuckin' stupid.

Honesty

When I was twenty-two, I finally got my first job running a club. It was owned by my mom's boyfriend, who was a well-to-do cat and a really nice guy. He knew that I'd been trying to get my own place after working in the bar business for four years, so when he asked me if I wanted to be his night manager, I gave my usual answer: "Hell, yeah!"

That place had one bar, with two or three bartenders behind the stick and a band down at the end. There was a restaurant upstairs that stopped serving at ten, and the bar downstairs would go all night. It took some adjustment because it was a small room, and I was used to workin' in really big places. I mean, the bar where we had that biker fight had forty-four bouncers—we were like a gang!

The main reason I liked big places was because you could have pussy all over the room, you could have five girls goin' at the same time. But now, I'm at this small bar, maybe 1,200 square feet, and you can't work two or three girls like that. Well, not unless you try something that I'd never tried before—HONESTY. Bro, I got so honest with the girls, it was ridiculous, and as a result I got laid more than I ever had in my life!

Chasin' tail was the main thing for me back then, because I never thought of my jobs in nightclubs as real jobs. They were paying me to have fun, and of course to get laid! Man, those were some pretty great years!

🐦 *@RealDDP*

🌐 *www.DiamondDallasPage.com*

🌐 *www.DDPYoga.com*

Chapter Eighteen

'THE QUEEN OF SPADES'
SHAYNA BASZLER

Photo courtesy Shannon Knapp (InvictaFC.com).

"There's certain social rules that guys usually follow, but with girls, all bets are off. There's no rules."

One of the most charismatic and exciting fighters in the sport of MMA, "The Queen of Spades" Shayna Baszler is also one of the primary architects of the North American women's division.

A Muay Thai kru (teacher), Brazilian jiu-jitsu brown belt and advanced-level catch wrestling practitioner, Baszler boasts a skill set and track record that make her a standout among both fans and peers.

Also a massive fan of pro wrestling, Shayna holds the "Arn Anderson" role in the Ronda Rousey-led (and pro wrestling-inspired) "Four Horsewomen" MMA faction.

With a hard-fought record forged in the United States, Japan and Costa Rica, Baszler stands as one of the last holdovers from MMA's "anyone, anytime, anyplace" era.

"Worthless" Move

I occasionally help out the bouncing crew at a club in South Dakota called The Vault. They call me in for special events to help with females and keep legal stuff off their back. A lot of the females [who come in] know that the male bouncers aren't going to go into the women's restroom, so if they start having a beef with each other, they'll go there to fight. So that's where a lot of my work is.

In my experience, women are a lot more ruthless than men in their altercations. There's certain social rules that the guys usually follow—like they're not gonna kick each other in the nuts, or they're not gonna pull each other's hair—but with girls, all bets are off. They're gonna hit with their purse, pull hair, whatever they can do. There's no rules.

So anyway, about a year ago I was working with The Vault's crew at an outdoor festival at the fairgrounds in Sioux Falls, and I ended up learning a little lesson in humility when it comes to doubting traditional martial arts. You see, I used to take hapkido-type classes where they taught weapon disarms, and at those classes they taught us this move against somebody who is trying to downward-stab you in the top of the skull. You know, like they do in a scary slasher movie.

I remember learning this disarm and being like, "This move is worthless! Realistically, who's ever gonna chase you with a knife [while] stabbing the air like this? This is a worthless move!" My friend and I used roll our eyes every time we had to drill it, and we'd always joke about how it was the lamest move in martial arts.

So I was at the festival and a fight broke out, and they radioed me to come and escort this, um, larger black woman out. When I got there she was pretty fired up, and had one of her high-heeled shoes in her hand. Then as I tried to control her, she held up that shoe and GAVE ME THE SLASHER MOVE WITH IT! I couldn't believe it—she was bringing that heel down on my head in EXACTLY the way we'd always practiced!

I guess if you drill something often enough, it gets into your muscle memory even when you're making fun of it, because without even thinking I used the hapkido disarm and it worked like a charm. Pulled that shoe right out of her hand and hustled her off the property.

When I got off work that night, I had to shamefully call my friend and take back everything I said about it being the most worthless move ever. It almost made me mad [to admit it]. "Dammit, it's real! We can't make fun of it anymore!" (laughs)

🐦 *@QoSBaszler*

Chapter Nineteen

ROB ARCHER

Photo by Andre Rowe.

"One minute you're having a normal night, and the next you're getting ready to go home with some chick you've only seen in porn videos."

It's hard to argue with Rob Archer's claim to being "the world's largest in-shape stuntman". Standing six foot six and weighing a shredded two hundred ninety pounds, Archer has a lock on most of the "giant freak" roles in Toronto's movie and TV industry.

His recurrent portrayals of Bioman Ulysses on the TV show *Defiance,* and the hulking Bruce on the series *Lost Girl*, along with

numerous appearances in big-budget movies like *Kick-Ass 2*, have gar-
nered Rob a steadily-growing fanbase and brought him well beyond
his days of looming over the doorways of clubs all over the East Coast.

Face Plant

Man, I've bounced all over the place. Strip clubs, roadhouses, nightclubs, whatever. I've worked everywhere and seen everything—
people getting sliced open, people ODing, people fucking and doing
drugs right out in the open. After a while, it just becomes another
day at work.

One of the grossest things I ever saw was in Fort Lauderdale
[Florida]. I was working the front door when this drunk guy staggered up with a face like raw hamburger. He had face-planted onto
broken glass, and taken almost his entire nose off! It was just holding
on by a little piece of nostril skin, and you could see right up into his
skull, cartilage and everything. I couldn't believe the guy was still
standing, but I guess he was so inebriated that he didn't know his
nose was hanging off his face.

I sat him down on the curb, and called my manager to come and
take care of the guy until we could get an ambulance. As far as I was
concerned, situations like that weren't part of my job description, so
I wasn't going to touch that bloody mess!

The Abyss

Something even worse happened a couple of years earlier in
Mississauga [Ontario], at this incredibly violent place called The
Abyss. I got a "Code White" call, which meant that something

bad was going down on the dance floor. I ran over there to see that the floor, which was supposed to be blue, now had a ten-by-ten-foot section that was completely red with blood. It was like a horror movie, everybody in the area was covered in splatter.

Two dudes had gotten into it—over a girl, of course—and one of them had shoved a broken bottle into the other's arm and hit an artery. The guy who got stabbed almost died right there on the dance floor. They rushed him to the nearest hospital, and then had to helicopter him to a more advanced facility. I still don't know if he lived.

The amount of fights and stupid shit I've seen, especially over girls, is unbelievable. People just don't think. They get their emotions up, and all of a sudden they've done something in five seconds that will cost them five years, ten years, maybe the rest of their life in jail. So stupid.

Fighting Without Fighting

One thing I'm very proud of is that in my entire bouncing career, I never punched a single person. Not that I didn't want to at times, but I quickly realized that no matter what somebody came at me with—a knife, a broken bottle, whatever—if I hurt them and I went to court, the judge was going to look at my size and I'd be automatically guilty. So it was always choke holds, headlocks, or else I'd just throw them down, but I always knew that I couldn't leave marks no matter what. After all, it wasn't like I could say "It wasn't me, it was one of the other guys," because nobody else looked like me. We live in a suing generation, people will try to irk bouncers just so they can sue them. So to a lot of guys, I was an obvious target.

I remember an incident in late 2011, when a black guy at the front door was really antagonizing me, even calling me a "nigger." Because, you know, that's the perfect way to describe a giant, inked white guy with a shaved head who looks like a member of the Aryan Nations, right? (laughs) I was still trying to figure this guy out when I noticed an Escalade across the street with four or five of the dude's fellow thugs in it, all watching and waiting to do me in.

Suddenly this wasn't just a matter of legalities anymore, it was a matter of self-preservation. No matter how big I might be, I'm not bigger than five guys who may or may not be armed. So instead of getting violent, I just decided to make the guy look stupid in front of everybody. I said, "I don't know if you noticed son, but I'm not a 'nigger.' And I'm also not the one stuck outside of this club." Then I turned my back, walked inside, and he didn't have shit to say. I wanted to kick his ass SO BADLY, but I knew that this was one of those times when putting my hands on someone was just not an option.

A smart bouncer always realizes that he is a disposable hero. The club managers will feed you bullshit—"You're the best! We love you here!"—but the very second you become a liability, either by hurting someone or getting hurt, they will cut you loose and not give a fuck about you. You have to be your own protector because they won't spend a nickel to save your ass.

Gentlemen's Clubs

I was a few years into my bouncing career when I started running security at high-end gentlemen's clubs, first in Toronto, and then in Fort Lauderdale. That was one of the best career moves I ever made because the money was just insane. People would come to the front door, shake your hand, and they'd slip you one hundred, two hundred bucks to get

Rob in the midst of being "BioManned" on the set of DEFIANCE. Photo courtesy Rob Archer.

them a good table, and bring them the best girls so they could impress their buddies or clients.

It always amazed me that they would drop literally thousands of dollars on the girls, but never seem to realize that it was the bouncers and hosts who were fucking them! (laughs) At one place in Florida, I was dating one of the dancers and a high-roller asshole found out. So he came up to me with a smirk on his face, and said, "Your girl danced for me last night." But instead of getting pissed, I just shook his hand with a big smile, and said, "That's great! Because you see these pants I'm wearing? You paid for them! And you also paid the bill at the fancy restaurant we went to last night. So thank you, bro... and please feel free to get some more dances from her tonight!" (laughs)

Hook-Ups

Speaking of women, I have to say that they were one of the absolute best things about the job. Not just regular customers either. I'm talking bartenders, waitresses, strippers—and the hook-ups could happen so quickly! One minute you're having a normal night, and the next you're getting ready to go home with some chick who you've only seen in porn videos. It's like, "How the shit did this happen?" (laughs)

It was always easy for me, because most of the nightlife girls want a piece of the biggest, most inked-up guy in the club, either because they're obsessed with muscle and tats, or just because they're curious to see if all the parts measure up. (laughs)

But all that action does kind of ruin you for the normal world, because once you leave the nightlife and try to meet a normal girl, it's like eating vanilla ice cream every night. You know, "What's it gonna be tonight, missionary or missionary?" (laughs) You spend seventeen years with all these crazy chicks, doing all kinds of fucked-up shit, and then you try to do normal and it's really boring.

Gene Simmons

One of my favorite gigs ever was doing personal security for Gene Simmons and Shannon Tweed. It was after I'd moved back to Toronto, and they were in town to visit the Toronto International Film Festival and shoot an episode of their *Family Jewels* show at the Tattoo Rock Parlour on Queen Street.

Now, with a lot of celebrities, what you see is all image. The persona they show the public is not who they really are. For instance, Steven Seagal always talks like he's this spiritual guy, but he's probably the biggest Hollywood asshole you'll ever meet. But on the other side of things, Gene Simmons was probably the coolest and nicest guy I've ever met in my life.

The whole day, the crowds were crazy, and I had to stay on Gene and Shannon like glue. It was insane, people were crushing forward and going crazy trying to touch him. But several times throughout that day, whenever we got a quiet moment, he would turn to me and say stuff like, "Thank you so much, you're handling this amazingly. I really appreciate it." No matter how intense and stressful things got, he was just incredibly cool and polite all day long.

It was so great to work with a celebrity who's even cooler in person than he is on his show, and that day was definitely one of the highlights of my career in security.

Looking Back

I'm out of the industry now, and I have to say that I've grown to hate the nightlife. That scene is like Cinderella—it's a fairy tale, it's not real. I used to just stand back and watch all these guys who had prettier eyebrows than the girls they were telling lies to, and all these little girls who couldn't even walk properly in their high heels, leeching onto whatever guy would feed them the biggest amount of bullshit. And of course, there were the ever-present drunk guys, always coming up to ask me how much I bench or whatever, just so they could go back to their friends and brag about talking to the big scary guy. It was, and still is, so fucked.

I can't even relax in that environment anymore, or at any gathering of people for that matter. Even if I'm just at a birthday party, my back is against the wall and I'm watching everything that's going on. That comes from seventeen years of being under constant physical threat, and now when I go back and visit my friends who are still bouncers, I'll stay in the street in front of the club. You couldn't pay me to go inside.

I won't say that it was never fun, or that I never enjoyed the work, but I'm happy that those days are long gone. Today, I love my job in the film industry and I appreciate it more than anything. I could win the lottery tomorrow, and I'd still show up for work and put in eighteen-hour days with a smile. I mean, my final job of last year was having a gunfight with Robocop! How fucking cool is that?

It's like I'm getting my payoff for all that time in bars and night-clubs. I finally found my happy ending, and I'm never looking or going back.

@BigInkdArcher

Chapter Twenty

PATRICK GALLAGHER

All photos courtesy Patrick Gallagher.

> *"I went out there and started mocking him, 'Oh my God, you're so manly!' Ten minutes later, he came back and showed me a gun in his waistband."*

Dividing his time between Los Angeles and Vancouver, prolific actor Patrick Gallagher has amassed an impressive body of work that includes prominent roles in the TV series *Glee* and *True Blood*, and the *Night at the Museum* film series.

But success has not erased his memories of his early days in the streets of Toronto, where he did his best to keep from being maimed or killed while getting his acting career out of the gate.

RPM

RPM was a famous club on Queen's Quay in Toronto. It changed its name to The Guvernment later on, and now I believe it's closed down. I was there around '93 or '94 and I started working on the floor. Then I got moved out to the front door, and would only go inside if other bouncers needed help.

In the winter, it would get cold as fuck out there, so cold that my legs would really hurt. After a few weeks, someone told me that panty hose would help with leg support and insulation. I wasn't sure if they were ribbing me, but I was desperate enough to try anything. And the person wasn't lying, it worked! Support hose kick ass to keep your legs warm. Of course, my very first night wearing 'em I was up in some guy's face, telling him that he was looking to get his ass kicked, and I couldn't help but think how I was acting the tough guy with panty hose on under my long johns! Thank God nobody knew, because who's gonna listen to a bouncer who wears panty hose? But I wanna stress that I never wore fishnets. Make sure you write that down, "No fishnets."

That place could be a tough one to work, especially when they had live bands. The Rolling Stones once played a short-notice gig there, and it was an all-day, all-night mob scene. When the Wu-Tang Clan played, we had thirty-five doormen for only 200 patrons, but the crowd was so rough that we still felt understaffed. And The Four Horsemen... oh my fucking God. Every time they came around, it was insanity! On the upside, their fans only fought with their fists, so there was no gunplay or anything. But it would literally be one getting thrown out after another, all night long. Every one [that we threw out] was angry, wasted, violent, and wanting to come back in. One drunken asshole even picked up a ten-foot-long sawhorse barricade and tried to swing it at me. But he fell on his ass with the barricade on top of him, which brightened my evening quite a bit.

Working The Door

I always showed respect to everyone who showed it to me, because I never agreed with treating people like cattle. That's why I wouldn't do that fake-line bullshit, where you have nobody inside but you make people wait out front so it looks busy. I'd always tell people, "If I'm working and you see a line, it's because we're legitimately full."

When we did have a line, it amazed me how some people thought that acting like a dick would get them in quicker. One night, I had a guy who was just on me, rudely trying to talk his way in and never letting up. Every time I'd let someone in, he'd be like, "How come they get to go in?" and I'd say, "Because they were polite and they kept their mouth shut." But he never got it, and as a result, he never got in.

Another thing that pissed me off was people showing up drunk at the front door, as if I wasn't gonna notice that they reeked of booze and couldn't stand straight. I'd ask how many drinks they'd had, and they'd hold up three fingers and say "Four!" Sometimes, if they were right on the edge and it was a judgment call, I'd ask historical questions like, "What's the significance of Vimy Ridge?" You know, doing my bit to educate the younger generation. But very few people could answer my questions. So sad.

I'll never forget the time a guy got to the front of the line and he could barely stand up. I wouldn't let him in no matter how much he begged, and I told him over and over that no way was he getting in in his condition. Finally, somebody pulled me aside and told me that the guy had cerebral palsy! That was bad, I felt really awful. But what was I supposed to do? He looked drunk!

I loved it when people said, "I just wanna see my friend, I'll be ten minutes" and then they'd stay in there forever. I'd take their wallet as collateral, and tell them, "If you're late, I'm throwing it in the garbage." Then they'd come out an hour later and be shocked that I actually did it. Hey, it's not like I didn't warn you, dude—now go dig through the garbage and find your wallet.

Also, to any ladies who might be reading this, don't think that a smart bouncer's gonna let you in because it's fifteen below and you CHOSE not to wear a coat. We have a coat check in the bar, and you weren't forced to come here dressed like that. Now get your ass back in line and borrow your boyfriend's coat or something, because I ain't buyin' it.

Stuck-Up Bitches

One of the worst parts of the job was dealing with the stuck-up bitches—and I want to stress that "bitch" is a word I only use to describe women who earn it. They'd always walk around like their looks made them better than everybody else. Don't get me wrong, there were some gorgeous women who came in and were totally cool, but I used to love messing with the stuck-up ones. They would walk straight to the front of the line and just expect to get in, but I'd act confused and say, "But ladies, you've already been in... oh wait... I'm sorry, my mistake. It's just that you look exactly like every other girl in the place." (laughs) They HATED that! And if they had especially bad attitudes, I'd say, "Sorry girls, but *yesterday* was 'No Cover for Girls Who Spend Two Hours Making Themselves Look Like Prostitutes.' Too bad you missed it, we had drink specials."

Talking Myself Out Of Trouble… And Into It

When customers got thrown out, my attitude was always to try to get on their side right away. You know, say stuff like, "You're right bro, that doorman who threw you out was an asshole." Of course I didn't believe that, but it was all psychology. I figured my job was to keep them from coming back in, and if I could do that without throwing a punch, then so much the better.

Sometimes, I could even understand where they were coming from, even when their anger was directed at me. After all, we've all been that guy calling somebody an asshole outside a bar at one time or another. I never really cared what people called me, as long as it wasn't racial. Call me most other things and I don't give a shit, I'll just laugh. But racial shit drives me crazy.

I have to admit that there were some times that I couldn't help myself, and I'd be the one saying stupid shit. If a guy had been a real problem, then while he was getting into a cab I'd say "By the way, tell your mother I want my underwear back." Then he'd go crazy while I laughed my ass off. I did feel bad for the taxi drivers, because every asshole we threw out of the club was getting into a taxi, and I probably made things worse for those drivers. But I eventually got mine when I pulled that routine with the wrong guy.

You know those big, round, plastic road pylons? The striped ones that look like barrels? Well, this dude we kicked out was throwing them around—taking out his frustration on 'em I guess—and I went out there and started mocking him. I'd go to pick one up, but pretend it was too heavy, and say "Oh my God, you're a fucking superman! I can't even lift it! You're so manly!" Eventually he stopped, looked at me, and walked away.

Ten minutes later, he came back and showed me a gun in his waistband.

I feel no shame in saying that I immediately put a brick wall between me and that gun. But our head doorman Carl, he didn't give a fuck. He marched out there, walked right up to the guy and said, "C'mon, motherfucker, if you're gonna do it, do it." Carl obviously had a good sense that the guy wasn't going to pull the trigger, but still, that's not a risk I would've wanted to take. Thank God the guy thought better of it and went home.

Riot At The Satellite

The gun incident convinced me to look for a safer place to work, so I jumped over to The Satellite Lounge, which was located in the upstairs of the Atlas Bar & Grill on the corner of Peter and King.

I was told that it was a less violent place than RPM, so I began working the door with a five-foot-six British guy named Steve, who was a chippy little dude who liked to head-butt people. He was good at it too, because he was so short that he'd always get 'em right in the nose. He immediately liked working with me because I was a good talker and could calm people down—and by "people", I mean "Steve." He even told me one night, "Fuck the customers, your main job is to keep me from head-butting anybody."

Steve and I never took money to let people in—which in retrospect, I see as a mistake—but we did accept tips in the form of Jack-and-Cokes, so we were almost always a little tipsy. Neither one of us had a radio, so we never got notice of anything happening inside the club until it dropped in our laps on the way out. One night, after Steve had gone inside to help with a situation, I saw this big scuttlebutt coming down the stairs. I figured that, like always, it was only gonna be three or four guys, but people just kept coming and coming and coming.

All of a sudden, I'm in the middle of a bona fide gang fight.

I found out later that one of the guys who started it had been hitting on a bouncer's Asian girlfriend, and when she blew him off, the guy made a racial slur. He made the horrible mistake of doing it with Steve standing beside him, and one head-butt later, it was ON. Everybody spilled into the street, and the fighting was vicious. The whole block looked like a war zone—blood on the sidewalk, wounded bodies everywhere, a guy running down the street with a pen stuck in his eye—even the guy who ran the hot dog cart out front was waving a machete! It was chaos, I have no idea how I lived through that.

Finally, it kind of wore off to the point that everybody could take a breath. The bad guys were lined up in the street, and we were lined up on the sidewalk facing them. It was looking like we were almost done, like we were just gonna jaw at each other until the cops showed up, but then one of the guys looked at me and said, "You fat Chink!"

Now, as I told you before, I lose my mind over racial shit. So I looked at Steve and said, "Steve, he just said the word. May I?" And Steve did a little bow, held out his hand, and said, "Be my guest."

I stepped into the street, walked right up to the guy, and told him, "I may be fat, but I have never been and never will be a Chink!" And then I NAILED him in the mouth with the only premeditated punch I ever threw as a bouncer. Of course, that kicked everything off all over again.

The cops finally showed up in force, and we ended up having to go to court three times because there was racial stuff involved, and

Patrick as Attila the Hun in the NIGHT AT THE MUSEUM series.

the prosecutors insisted on classifying it as a hate crime. But nothing came of it in the end, and all the charges on both sides got dropped. That was fine by me—I got to punch that guy in the head, so I was okay with leaving it there.

Rich Assholes

I used to love kicking assholes out of the Atlas. In spite of that one riot, it was a much higher-end clientele than RPM, so the worst you could usually expect was some yuppie lawyer screaming "Don't touch me, I'll sue you." Whenever I got that, I'd just tap the guy on the shoulder and say, "There, you just made a million dollars." And then I'd throw him out anyway.

My favorite thing to do when a wealthy jerk started shooting his mouth off, was to ask him how pissed off he was. "How much does this situation bother you, sir? You make more in a day than I do in a year, but I'm saying 'No' and you can't do a damn thing about it. How much does that piss you off?" It got to be a game, seeing how crazy I could make them.

"I'm gonna buy this place and fire you!"

"Okay, please do that. I hate this fucking job."

Drove 'em nuts.

Game Over

I eventually quit bouncing after getting a very loud wake-up call from, of all people, a teenage kid. He walked up to me off the street and said, "I'm only fourteen years old, so I could shoot you right now and nothing would happen. I'd get maybe eighteen months in juvie, and that would be it." And I thought, "Damn, he's right and he knows it!" Right there, I decided say goodbye to the bouncing life. I missed the money for a while until my acting career took off, but hey, who wants to get shot to death for twelve bucks an hour?

🐦 *@PatrickGMan*

Chapter Twenty-One

JOHN 'THE MACHINE' LOBER

All photos courtesy John Lober.

"I've got one guy by the neck, one guy by the shirt, and I'm knee-dropping the third one in the face."

During the mid-to-late 90s, John "The Machine" Lober was an extremely prominent figure on the MMA landscape. After making his MMA debut at IFC 1 in Kiev, Ukraine, Lober became notorious for defeating former King of Pancrase Frank Shamrock in Shamrock's closed-fist MMA debut (famously pulling his own damaged front teeth out at the end of the fight). An intense rivalry ensued that led to one of the most anticipated rematches in the sport, a 1998 battle over Shamrock's Ultimate Fighting Championship title in the first UFC event ever held on Brazilian soil.

As a man who once fought ten times in two years, and has battled on four continents, John Lober stands as a living embodiment of the "for the love of the fight" ethos of modern MMA's early days.

Margaritaville

While I have worked as a bouncer before, I've never been considered much of a bouncer or security force—not in the professional sense. I'm more the guy who's gonna take everybody down and ask questions later. Basically, if you say "bouncing," I automatically think "fighting."

In the [early 90s] before I got into MMA, my only training came from street fighting. Almost every night, bro—if there was a night when I wasn't in a fight, I was looking for a party so I could find a fight. Get drunk, get in a fight, get laid—that was pretty much what my life revolved around at the time.

Around 1995, I was working occasionally at a place called Margaritaville in Newport Beach [California]. My buddy [UFC veteran] Todd Medina used to work at the front door, and he'd hire me every once in a while. The job paid $150 for the night, so it was a pretty good deal. This was just after Kimo [Leopoldo] beat up Royce [Gracie at UFC 3], and Kimo was a local guy, so there was a real UFC buzz going around. I actually grew up watching Kimo beat guys up at a place called Mazzotti's on Main Street in Huntington Beach. I think it's a police substation now, but back in the day that place was a battlefield. I used to just watch the criminals and gangsters beat each other up every weekend, before the city finally cleaned the whole area up.

So one night I'm working and Todd isn't there. It's me and a guy named Craigie—who was around six foot five and two-eighty—on the front door. Craigie gets into it with some guy, grabs the guy by the neck, and then three of the guy's buddies jump in. So I get into it with them, and the whole thing spills out into the street. I've got one guy by the neck, one guy by the shirt, and the third guy is on the ground and I'm knee-dropping him in the face over and over. It's funny, even though I'm not a huge guy—about five eleven and one-eighty—I've always been more comfortable fighting multiple opponents. For some reason, it just seems easier to me.

Anyway, I'm just blasting the guy on the ground with my knee because I don't want him to get up, you know? And as all this is going on, I look up and see this chick looking out the window from inside the bar. It's funny the things you notice in the middle of a fight—I can clearly read her lips as she says, "What an ASS-HOLE!" (laughs) Thankfully, I never cared about winning any popularity contests, so I just carry on and beat the shit out of the other two guys as well.

A couple of minutes later, the Newport Beach cops roll up, and the three guys I pummeled go running up to the cruiser. I'm thinking I'm gonna get busted for sure, but the cop just looks at them, looks at me, and says, "No way did *that* guy do this to all three of you by himself! Get the fuck out of here!" Then he gets back in his car and takes off! (laughs) That was awesome.

Going To Jail

About a year later, I had just beat a guy named Jamie Fawcett on an IFC show in Mississippi, and I was out with my friends celebrating. We were at a club called Kirk's, and everybody was on mushrooms and shit—not me though—and some guy stepped on my toe and then slapped me on the head! So I uppercutted him, and the bouncers surrounded me and ran me outside. But I took out a bunch of them too, so they ran back inside and shut the door, locking me and a training buddy of mine outside.

We knew we weren't gonna get back in, so we just said, "fuck it" and went to another bar. But we had barely ordered our drinks when the cops pulled up and arrested me! That was the first time I was ever arrested for fighting, but I couldn't complain because with all the stuff I'd done over the years, making it into my thirties before finally getting arrested was pretty good! (laughs) I got sentenced to ten days of Caltrans [highway road crew], but I fucked that off and took twenty-two days in jail instead because I needed the rest! (laughs) It ended up being not bad at all—the guards were all superfans and they knew who I was, so all I did was mow lawns the whole time I was there.

Lober (right) with his greatest rival,
five-time UFC Champion Frank Shamrock.

The Last Time

Once in 2009, this guy asked me to come and bounce with him at a club in Newport Beach. I kept telling him that I wasn't into it, but he wouldn't let it go. "C'mon, I need you. I'll get you a suit, all you have to do is stand there." I finally gave in and agreed, but when he came to pick me up, my chick looked at me and said, "It's not a good idea." (laughs) But I went anyway.

At one point, I'm standing outside the club and the guy I'm working with says, "I have to go inside for a minute. Don't let anyone in because we're full." Of course, he's barely been gone a minute when a bunch of Persian guys roll up. They're all blasted on cocaine, drunk, shirts unbuttoned with their chest hairs hangin' out and shit, and acting like they own the place.

I tell them that we're full, but then another HUGE Persian guy comes out of the club, and it's the same deal with this guy—greasy hair, shirt unbuttoned, hairy chest with gold chains, high as fuck on cocaine. He looks at me and says, "Don't worry about it, they're with me." But I tell him, "I don't care who they're with, they're not allowed in."

He just looks at his friends and says, "Don't worry about this guy," and then pushes me aside and unhooks the velvet rope! I say again, "Dude, they're not supposed to go in," and then the guy SNAPS! He grabs one of the poles that hold the rope up, and throws it at my head! It misses, and then the manager and the guy I was working with both come running out. For the next couple of minutes, everybody's pushing and shoving and yelling, and it's just a mess.

I finally get to where I've had enough, so I walk up to the guy who threw the pole, punch him right in the face and knock him out. Then I look at the manager and say, "There, it's solved. I quit." (laughs) I call my chick and tell her to pick me up across the street, and her timing is perfect because the cops come rolling in just as we're pulling away.

So really, I'm not much of a bouncer. I'm happy to leave all that shit to the people who have the patience for it.

🐦 *@JTLober*

Chapter Twenty-Two

PAUL 'POLAR BEAR' VARELANS

Photo courtesy Susumu Nagao.

"I don't remember biting him, but I'm not gonna say it didn't happen. All I can say in my own defense is that Russian vodka is GOOD."

More than fifteen years after his last fight, UFC veteran Paul "Polar Bear" Varelans remains a captivating figure for hardcore MMA fans. After making his debut in 1995 at the appropriately-named *UFC 6: Clash of the Titans,* the monstrous Alaska native rattled off eighteen fights over a three-year career that took him to Brazil, Holland, Japan and the Ukraine. His gargantuan size, and epic clashes with warriors like Tank Abbott, Kimo, and Mark

"The Smashing Machine" Kerr made Varelans a highly sought-after audience favorite.

While I was always a Varelans fan, he became a permanent favorite of mine on the night that he utilized his surprisingly top-notch diplomatic skills to save me and a number of others from being shot by Nigerian gangsters on a Tokyo sidewalk. But that's a story for another time—for now, I present to you THE POLAR BEAR!

Dealing With Dicks

I first started bouncing while playing football in college. I don't think I was supposed to work, but I needed to because my scholarship wasn't paying shit. So I started at this Latin club in east Palo Alto [California], and I quickly got to be really good at what I did. My favorite methods [of dealing with problem customers] were all verbal. Anger and stupidity need momentum, and I found that if you interrupt that momentum by putting a thought in a guy's head that makes him stop and think about the bad things that could happen, he often backs off.

But of course, that didn't work on everybody. There were always the guys who wanted to take it too far, and you had to take 'em out. In my heyday, I was as good at doing that as I was at talking. I got to where I could overhand throw a guy and put a nice spin on him while he was in the air. If I wanted a dude out the door, but I also wanted him to bank off a wall and land on a specific spot on the ground, I could make it happen ten times out of ten.

It surprised me when guys wouldn't take instruction, because I could never figure out how they thought they were gonna win. I mean, at six foot eight and three-fifty, I wasn't really giving them a lot of physical options. Most guys knew that right off the bat, but there was still always that one guy who wanted to try. Man, I remember cases where a guy would be getting in my face, and *his own friends* would beat the crap out of him and tell the guy, "Better us than him!" (laughs)

Some guys would put a little more thought into it, and try to even the odds with a gun or a knife—because c'mon, no normal-sized guy is gonna come at me barehanded. So I prepared for that by doing a ton of knife training, especially disarms. Once I got a guy's knife away from him, I'd do what my mom always told me and put my toy back where I found it. Usually in the guy's thigh or something.

Bottle To The Face

One night, I got into it with a bunch of dudes—six or seven of 'em, I think—but it wasn't a problem because I had lots of practice with groups. It always seemed to be me against a bunch of guys. The only one-on-one fights I had were in the UFC.

It was going fine for a while, but I didn't see that one of the guys was holding a beer bottle, and he spun around with a spinning back fist—or spinning back bottle, I guess—that connected in my mouth and opened my lip right up.

That was a huge mistake, because the moment the blood hit my tongue, I lost it. I introduced his head to a brick wall a couple times, and then completely massacred the rest of 'em. That's not as hard as it sounds, because guys who fight in packs are cowards. Once you destroy the first one, once you leave him as a pile of broken bones in his own skin, the rest of 'em fold up like card tables.

After it was over, the guys who ran the club got me out the back door before the cops came. They also hooked me up with a doctor to give me stitches, so I wouldn't have to go to the hospital and deal with the police.

The Kit Kat Club

When I got into the UFC, I figured I was finished working in nightclubs. But then states started banning [MMA], which came at a really bad time for me. Fighting in the UFC was something I was really passionate about, but just when I felt like I was hitting my stride, the whole thing got yanked out. So without a job in the Octagon, I had to find a way to make money, and I was forced to go back [to bouncing].

I went to work at a strip joint in Sunnyvale, California called The Kit Kat Club. The owner of that place was the cheapest guy in the world—nobody got in for free. And I mean NOBODY got in for free. NO. BODY. I'd say it again, but you get the picture. For example, around that time a local band called Smashmouth was huge, but the owner wouldn't even allow us to let *them* in! In cases like that, I didn't like being the bad guy, but I also liked my $200 in tips every night, so I had to do what the boss wanted.

During my first week at that place, we had a group of about sixteen guys try to bum-rush the entrance. Since there were only three or four of us working, I got the call to come up from the back, and when I got out there, I just started grabbing dudes and chucking them. At one point, a guy tried a double-leg takedown, but of course I just stood there because I was too big for him to get me off my feet. All of a sudden, I felt his teeth digging into my thigh—and that was a big mistake [because] now we've moved from, "We're just gonna wrestle and have a good time" to "Do you have hepatitis, HIV, or something else that I have to worry about?" So I immediately went from proactive mode to reactive mode.

I leaned over, wrapped my arms around his waist, and threw the guy straight up into the air. At that point, everybody actually stopped fighting, and they just stood there watching this guy go up, and up, and up. He flew so high that I actually had time to think, "Oh shit, maybe I overdid it." (laughs) Then he came down, and that's when I found out why they call us bouncers, because with the right acceleration and the right landing points, the human body really does bounce quite nicely!

The guy hit the ground HARD and immediately started to bleed out. He was seriously a mess. Soon, we had an ambulance on the scene, and then the Sunnyvale Police Department came screeching up and started screaming at me to get on the ground. So now, I'm face-down on the ground and they're slapping the cuffs on me and taking pictures of the crime scene, and I'm thinking, "I'm fucked."

But then the captain of the watch drove up and got out of his car, and I guess he was a UFC fan because he looked at me and yelled what sounded like the two greatest words in the world: "POLAR BEAR!" (laughs)

He looked at his guys and said, "Uncuff him! What happened?" and I said, "The guy tried to bite me!"

"Oh, he assaulted you, right?"

"Yeah, he assaulted me!"

"Well then, you were defending yourself!"

And just like that, it went from "I'm going to prison" to "I'm doing photo ops with the captain and the arresting officers." One of the cops even got some hot water and started pouring it on the pavement to wash all the evidence away! (laughs)

After Party in Kiev

This one happened on the night I fought in IFC 1 in the Ukraine. Almost all the fight shows over there were [promoted] by the mob, so afterwards, all of us fighters went out with Russian gangsters who took us to various clubs. Almost every club was named after an American city, and had a strip club, a nightclub, a restaurant and a bar all mixed into one place.

So we're at one of these places, and I'm on an upstairs level hanging out with [UFC and Pancrase champion] Bas Rutten, who did commentary for the show. Bas is a great guy, he's always been in my corner—at times almost literally. Sometimes at fight shows, he would send notes to my cornermen [during the fight] to help me deal with guys. Solid dude.

So we're drinking vodka and trading your standard fighter shit-talk back and forth, and Bas looks at me and goes, "I could knock you out with one kick." I'm like, "You couldn't even reach my chin, okay?" (laughs) So Bas puts his drink down and does that jumping splits thing that he does, and then he says, "Okay, maybe I couldn't reach your chin, but I could knock you down or drag you down, and *then* I kick you out!"

And just like that, it's on—we start wrestling right there in the middle of the bar. We're not mad or anything, but it's still serious because professional fighters wrestling in fun is like two normal guys having a fight to the death. At one point, I grab him in a bodylock from behind, and apparently I bite him right in the back. I seriously don't remember doing that, but I'm not gonna say it didn't happen. All I can say in my own defence is that Russian vodka is GOOD.

Anyway, I've got him in a bodylock and he puts a Kimura [arm-lock] on me and throws me over his hip. But there's a partition close to us, kind of like a low wall with the lower half [made of] brick, and the top half glass. And of course I go right through the glass part! It shatters everywhere, and Bas is laughing his ass off as I pick myself up off the ground. I'm laughing too, but as I go to throw a joking elbow strike at him, I see that my elbow is sliced wide open, with blood gushing everywhere!

Our flight home is leaving in the morning, but I obviously can't fly while I'm filleted open, so the Russian mob guys take me straight to the hospital. The one they took me to, I swear to God it had to be from the 1920s. NEVER go to a Russian hospital, dude—that shit is DECREPIT. Pieces of the walls falling off and stuff. It was so scary, scarier than any fight I've ever been in. The guy who ends up working on me—I never did find out if he was even a real doctor—he has this big fucking Chef Boyardee hat on! I ask him what the fuck is up with his hat, and his only explanation is, "Hat is for sanitary." He stitches me up, and it hurts so damn much thanks to the weak-ass painkillers they gave me.

I end up getting out of there and making it to the airport barely on time, and to this day I still have a three-inch scar on my elbow to remind me of the whole experience.

Damn Bas. (laughs)

April 1997: Me and the Polar Bear backstage at a Pancrase event in Tokyo Bay NK Hall.

Lober's Bachelor Party

During that trip, I met [John] Lober who was fighting on the show too, and shortly after that, we ended up together again in Japan. We became really tight friends after that, and when he eventually got engaged, he invited me to be his best man. Which of course meant that I had to take him out for his bachelor party the night before.

His wife was like, "You gotta promise me, no black eyes for the wedding," and I'm like, "Yeah okay, no problem." After all, how hard can it be? (laughs)

So we go to this strip club in LA, and I stay close to him the whole night, because if you know Lober, you know that the instant somebody starts fuckin' with him, he's knocking 'em clean out. But eventually I have to take a piss, and of course I'm nervous to leave him because, you know, he's Lober. But at the same time, I'm not going to invite him to come with me like we're girls, and have him knock ME out instead. So I just tell him, "Look, I gotta go piss. Just be cool, okay? Just give me ten seconds, I'll be back." And he tells me he's cool.

Right.

I get to the restroom, and I've barely gotten my dick out when I hear it go off—BOOM! BOOM! BOOM! Shit! I don't even get to piss, I just stuff my junk back in my pants and run out, where I see Lober handcuffed to a rail that runs along the front of the stage. He's got about ten bouncers surrounding him, which seems about right because that's how many it would take to get handcuffs on Lober! (laughs)

Then I see one of the bouncers beatin' on Lober while he's cuffed, so I roll up on them and yell, "Those cuffs better be off in ONE SECOND or I'm leveling this place to its fucking foundations! And when the cuffs come off, Lober gets to square up with Happy Boy here who likes to punch people while they're restrained! Now DO IT!"

I look around to see if anyone wants to argue, but every single bouncer is looking down at the ground as the manager comes running over to unlock Lober. Then they all just turn around and walk away while Lober gets his piece of the guy who was beating on him.

Of course, Lober ends up with a black eye, which results in his wife trying to give *me* one when I bring him home! (laughs)

@PaulVarelans

Chapter Twenty-Three

PAUL 'THE MAULER' LAZENBY

Photo by Kirk Caouette.

"As Jonny walked toward the three guys, he grabbed a low-flying june bug out of the air and ate it alive."

Yes, I did put myself in my own book. Shut up.

In my defense, this story is too fucking awesome to be left untold—and besides, I figure that anybody who has been punched inna face by the legendary Royce Gracie should be allowed to do whatever they want.

So there.

Revolution

In 1993, I was running security at a giant club called Revolution in Waterloo, Ontario. The place was MASSIVE—it was actually a converted roller rink, so the dance floor alone could hold more people than many clubs' entire buildings.

One night, me and my right-hand man Jonny got swarmed by about twenty douchebags. It was nasty as hell for a while, and we were lucky to survive with only cuts and bruises. In the aftermath, we resolved to hunt down the guy who'd instigated the whole thing—a big-nosed, rat-faced little coward named Vern Milano.

Before I go any further, I should give you the 411 on Jonny, who was basically a fucking nightmare. Five foot ten and two hundred thirty pounds of ugly muscle, with pasty-white skin and a pile of shaggy dreadlocks that made his head look like a mutant tarantula. Within a couple of weeks of my hiring him, the number of fights in the club dropped about twenty percent just because of how scary he looked.

But it wasn't just his appearance that did it—it was also the fact that Jonny was not right between the ears. This was a guy who truly did not give the tiniest of fucks. Once, I watched him walk out to the parking lot where three guys were waiting to murder him and, without even breaking stride, casually grab a low-flying june bug out of the air and eat it alive. After the three guys saw that, the situation was quickly resolved without a single punch being thrown.

One night, about a month after we had gotten swarmed, Jonny came up and told me that my guy on the door had spotted Vern in the lineup. Little fucker must have thought that enough time had gone by for us to forget what he did, but he was about to find out how wrong he was.

With a million witnesses everywhere, there wasn't much we could do without getting arrested, so I just went out and grabbed the little shit by the scruff of his collar. Then I marched him up and down the full length of the lineup, loudly announcing to everybody what a cowardly piece of shit he was. When I finished, I turned Vern over to Jonny, who took a fistful of Vern's shirtfront and leaned so close that they were almost touching noses.

With surprising calmness, Jonny said, "Vern, if you ever come back to this club, I'm gonna take your pants off and fuck you in the ass." Vern tried to say something in response, but Jonny cut him off. "No, seriously, Vern. I don't want you to think that this is just me trying to sound tough. I promise you, I SWEAR to you, if you come back here again, I am seriously going to take out my cock and fuck you in your asshole. Seriously. For real."

And then he sent the little bastard on his way.

Fast forward to a Friday about six weeks later, which puts us in the middle of summer. We're about halfway through the night when Jonny comes jogging across the club looking like the world's most disturbing little kid on Christmas morning. "Guess who I just saw standing at the bar?" he says. "VERN MILANO!" I had never seen him so happy, he looked like he was about to start jumping up and down and clapping his hands like a little girl.

By this point, I'd forgotten the ass-fucking threat, but even if I hadn't, I wouldn't have taken it seriously. I mean, that's the kind of shit that guys always say when they're trying to throw a scare into somebody, but who really means it?

Right?

So we walked up on Vern, Jonny grabbed him by the back of his scrawny neck, and we marched him off toward the club's back doors. Those doors led outside to an enclosed area that I called "Asshole Jail." It was surrounded by a chain-link fence with barbed wire on top that kept you from climbing out, and once the doors slammed shut behind you, you couldn't get back into the club either. I liked to throw obnoxious customers out there to settle them down, especially in the wintertime.

The crowd that night was well behaved, so there was nobody out there when Jonny kicked the door open and dragged Vern outside. I stayed inside, holding the door open a crack so that Jonny could get back in after what I presumed was gonna be a garden-variety ass-whupping.

And that's exactly what it looked like at first, as Jonny clamped on a rear-naked choke and quickly turned Vern's lights out. But things went rapidly sideways when he dropped Vern to the ground and started going for the little bastard's belt buckle.

Oh, fuck.

I hissed at Jonny to stop, but he either couldn't hear me or didn't give a shit. He yanked Vern's pants and tighty-whities down, then hiked the little bastard's hips up so he was on his face and knees, with his cheek to the gravel and his bare ass to the sky.

I was still wondering how to stop this (while being morbidly curious about how far Jonny would actually take it) when Jonny walked around behind Vern, pulled back a size ten Doc Marten, and field-goal punted that little bastard right square in his anus. BOOM! The still-unconscious Vern's face skidded along the gravel as he flattened out from the impact, and then Jonny reached into his hip pocket, pulled out a condom, unwrapped it, unrolled it, and carefully positioned it on the ground beside Vern's face. Finally, Jonny unzipped his fly and stood patiently behind Vern, waiting.

Vern awoke a minute later, and immediately let out a loud moan of pain as he reached back to his bruised balloon knot. Then his eyes fell on the condom and he FROZE. It took everything I had not to bust out laughing as he slowly looked over his shoulder at Jonny.

Wearing a smile so big it almost cut his head in half, Jonny zipped up his fly, shot Vern a wink, and walked back into the club.

Vern came through the door a minute later, his eyes riveted to the ground as he beelined for the front door.

We never saw him in Revolution again.

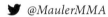 *@MaulerMMA*

Chapter Twenty-Four

JOHN RALLO

All photos courtesy John Rallo.

"When Ax Guy realizes he's on his own, he starts runnin' like hell from Ed who's gonna murder him with that bat."

Don't make the mistake of thinking that the tattoos and scowl are just a bluff. As nice a guy as he is, John Rallo is one of the LAST people you'd ever want to mess with.

With a combined sanctioned/unsanctioned MMA record of 6-1, and a Brazilian jiu-jitsu black belt earned from BJJ legend Renzo Gracie, Rallo brings plenty more to the table than just his giant slabs of bone-crushing muscle.

Also the man who got professional MMA sanctioned in the state of Maryland, Rallo currently promotes the wildly-popular Shogun Fights organization, runs the successful chain of Ground Control martial arts academies, and provides bodyguard services for a number of high-profile clients including Sylvester Stallone, Pamela Anderson, and Motley Crue drummer Tommy Lee.

The Harbor Inn

Back in the late 80s, when I was around eighteen, I worked at a club in Baltimore called The Harbor Inn. It was one of the hottest clubs in the state, and also one of the most violent. If you worked there five days a week, you were probably fightin' four out of the five. I once worked a New Year's Eve there and fought three times that night.

Funny enough, one of the craziest stories out of that place doesn't even involve a fight. I'm working on a Sunday, and this coke dealer named Mike comes in. In spite of his job, we didn't mind him comin' around because he didn't never start no trouble. He was as meek as could be, just a salesman. So after he's been in the club for a while, he comes up to where me and the boys are standing at the front door, and he says that there's a couple of dudes harassin' him.

So we go in there to give the guys a warning, and I see that one of the dudes is chewing off pieces of his glass and eating 'em! I guess that's supposed to scare me or something, but I don't give a shit. I tell 'em to hit the bricks, and we push 'em both out the front door without no trouble.

We go back to our spots at the door, and after a few minutes, I start hearing this pinging kind of noise. Next thing I know, a fuckin' window next to us shatters! So I yell, "We're gettin' shot at!" and we all hit the deck and army crawl back into the bar.

What those two dudes had done after we threw 'em out, they had drove about a hundred yards down the road onto an on-ramp for Route 895 that sat right above The Harbor Inn. They parked there, got out of the car, and set up with a small-caliber AK-47 clone, and then they started shootin' up the fuckin' parking lot!

Because the bullets were small, like .22s or something, you could hear them going *pyow* as they ricocheted off shit all over the place. The cops ended up finding a couple hundred rounds overall—they even found bullets in a building across the street! It was a real big deal, even made the news down here.

One of the scariest parts of this story is that while everything was happening, a cop named Paul Scardigna was parked behind a big limo in that lot, sitting in the driver's seat of his cruiser. They later found a bunch of bullets in the limo's roof, and when they checked the angle of the hits, they said that if that limo hadn't been there, Scardigna would have caught them bullets right in the chest!

Roughly a week later, Scardigna comes down to the bar with a bunch of mug-shot, line-up kinda pictures. He asks if I recognize anybody, and I point at a couple of the pictures and say, "Yeah, those two dudes are the ones we threw out." He goes, "Cool, that's all I needed. We got 'em."

He explains that after shooting up the parking lot, those guys went out whoring and bragged to a couple of hookers about what they did. Well, those girls must have had some kind of deal with the cops, because they dropped a dime the first chance they got. The girls even knew where the guys' car was stashed at, so the cops immediately located the car with the guns still in it, and picked up the guys shortly after.

Rallo with client and friend Tommy Lee.

Apparently, those dudes were sent up from Florida, and they obviously had some money behind 'em because a couple of high-priced lawyers had been at the police station trying to bail 'em out. Scardigna said he figured the dudes had been sent up specifically to do a hit on Mike the Coke Salesman. So basically, what started as a normal night at work ended up with a botched gangland execution! (laughs)

Lumberjacks

On another night, these two guys start fightin' and we yank 'em out the back door. In the process of this, one of 'em gets tough with one of our guys named Ed, and suddenly it's on between them two.

Now, we weren't the kind of crew who would have six bouncers stompin' one guy down. If it was one-on-one, the rest of us would stand back and let it play out. So Ed winds up whuppin' the shit outta this dude, and then it's over and done with, and we all go back to the front door.

Not even five minutes later a Chevy Blazer comes rippin' up, and out gets the guy Ed just pounded on—holding an ax! He starts chasin' Ed around the truck with it as two other guys jump out, so the rest of us run inside to a coatroom where we keep a bunch of aluminum bats for when crazy shit jumps off.

We grab the bats and run back outside, and I throw one of 'em to Ed. Without missin' a beat, Ed snatches that bat outta the air, spins around, and takes a vicious swing at Ax Guy's head. Lucky for Ax Guy, he's able to duck the swing, and Ed's follow-through smashes a window right out of the truck. The other two guys don't like that, so they're gone, and when Ax Guy realizes he's on his own, he starts runnin' like hell from Ed who's gonna murder him with that bat.

Wait a minute, it gets better.

Ax Guy starts runnin' up the road towards this street called Ponca Street, where there was a bunch of cars parked. There was also a bar up there called Partners where people would go when they left The Harbor Inn, and vice versa. He's runnin' towards one of the cars on Ponca, and suddenly two new guys who must have been friends of his jump out of it. They run around to the trunk, and I don't know if they was lumberjacks or what, but they pull CHAINSAWS out of the trunk and turn those motherfuckers on! So now you've got one guy with an ax and two guys with chainsaws against the six of us with aluminum bats.

Ax Guy winds up gettin' it first—he gets hit, he drops his ax, he gets fuckin' pelted with bats. Then we square off with the chainsaw guys. It's obvious from the way they're hangin' back that they're really just tryin' to scare us, but we ain't scarin'. We're like,

"Fuck you, motherfucker." Then one of the chainsaws stalls—and I don't think I have to tell you what happens after that. That guy's gettin' hit with like, four fuckin' bats, and his friend starts sprinting towards Partners while still holding a running chainsaw.

This is all goin' down in a rough industrial area—there's a roofing/shingle company across the street from us and shit—and as we chase this guy up Ponca Street, we come across an oven door lying by the side of the road. So my buddy Craig, who's like, three hundred and fifty pounds, he picks up that door and throws it like a fuckin' discus. Just LAUNCHES it. It spins through the air and hits the guy with the chainsaw—who's almost made it to Partners by now—hits him right in the back and knocks him down.

As the guy topples over, he loses his grip on the chainsaw, and it bounces right through the front door of Partners—STILL ON. Now people are screamin' and scatterin' out of there, and it's this guy's turn to get the shit beat out of him with bats because hey, he's no longer got a chainsaw. And that goes on until the police finally show up to close the show.

Partners ended up getting written up for the whole incident, and they were SO pissed off at us about it. The whole time they were like, "It was The Harbor Inn! It was them!" (laughs)

Man, half the times I tell that story, people don't believe it. But that kind of shit that used to happen to us all the time!

🐦 @jrallo44

🌐 www.ShogunFights.com

🌐 www.GroundControlBaltimore.com

Chapter Twenty-Five

'IRON BEAR' GARY MYERS

All photos courtesy Gary Myers.

> ***"She gimme a virgin, and I give her back
> a hellcat. But that's what you got when you
> trained with the Iron Bear!"***

An unsung pioneer of MMA, Indiana's "Iron Bear" Gary Myers went straight from a near-miss at the US Olympic wrestling trials to making history at the inaugural Battlecade Extreme Fighting tournament. During the wild, head-butt, bare-knuckle, stomp-a-grounded-opponent days of the 1990s, Gary compiled an official record of 14-10—and an unofficial record of God knows what—in bouts across the USA, Brazil, Russia, and Japan.

As the IWF world no-holds-barred tournament champion, a national wrestling champion and All-American, and the first heavyweight champion of the groundbreaking HOOKnSHOOT organization, the Iron Bear stands as one of the most savage and brutal fighters to come out of the American midwest.

Hot Shots

I want to start this off by saying that these are stories from my younger, wilder days. I'm now a God-fearing, respectable member of society, and I don't act like this no more! (laughs)

During the early 90s, I was bouncing in a place called Hot Shots in Muncie, Indiana. One night, there's a group of eleven guys hanging out there while I'm pickin' up these two black chicks—and doin' a good job of it, I might add. (laughs) But for whatever reason, that gets those guys all pissed off at me.

At the end of the night, the bar's cleared out and I go to walk the chicks to their car. The eleven guys are out in the parking lot by this point, and one of 'em says some shit to me as I walk by. So I just say "Fuck it", walk right into the middle of all of 'em, and start punching everybody I can. Get my lip busted pretty good, but I also knock three of 'em out cold.

The cops finally arrive, and since Muncie's not a big place, I know almost the whole department pretty good. They get out of their car and say "Bear, you got this under control?" and I say, "Hell yeah, I got it under control!" But then they look at the three bodies and say, 'Damn, we gotta call an ambulance." And that's when a couple of those sonsabitches I was fighting start yelling about pressin' charges. At that point, the cops have no choice but to take me into custody.

November 1995: Gary with Mr. T at Battlecade Extreme Fighting 1.

So the cuffs go on, and we all go to the hospital where the cops get these idiots looked at. I'm sittin' on a bench in this big room with my cuffs on and my bloody lip, and the three dudes I KOed are in beds, with their buddies standing all around. We're not there long before the police chief, a guy named Joe Winkel, walks in. He looks all around the room, then leans down real close to me and whispers, "Okay Bear, leave it to me, I'll see if I can smooth the situation over."

Then Joe straightens up, clears his throat and says, "Well, I'm just gonna say somethin' right here and now. It was Gary pickin' up two black girls that started this whole mess, and now I see an Indian guy, a white guy and a black guy all on gurneys. So whatever else you wanna say... at least Gary's not prejudiced!" (laughs)

Club Mark

A few years later in 1997, I was bouncing at a roadhouse on Stop Road in Indianapolis called Club Mark. I was doing it just for fun, since I was doing well in real estate and didn't really need the money.

During that time, I was living in a big house with just me in it, so I'd take in out-of-town fighters when they wanted to come down and train with the Indy fighters. Back then, MMA was still called NHB [No Holds Barred], and it was so new that it was hard to find other fighters to train with, so it wasn't unusual for guys to travel like that.

One day, I got a call from Phyllis Lee, my then-manager, who told me that she had this kid named Ryan Stout and she wanted me to show him the ropes. She said he was a good athlete who had some jiu-jitsu training, but warned me that he was also real innocent. Young kid, clean-cut, never been laid, never been drunk—you know the type. I had no idea why she thought it was safe to send a kid like that to me, but I told her to send him on by.

We arranged for him to meet me at work, and after he showed up at Club Mark, we shot the shit for a little bit. But he was barely there a half-hour when this big black guy walked in—had to be two hundred forty pounds, and solid—and said, "Who's Gary Myers?" I guess he knew my reputation from fighting on pay-per-view and overseas, but for some reason the dumb sumbitch couldn't pick me out of the crowd.

So I walked up and said, "I'm Gary" and he said, "I wanna fight you, let's go." Well, I was already kinda drunk and not really feelin' it, so I said, "I ain't gonna fight you." But then the guy pulled out a thick stack of cash, and said he wanted a winner-take-all fight. Right away, a buddy of mine pulled out a stack of his own to match it. So I said, "I still ain't gonna do it... but I have a kid over here named Ryan who'd be happy to take you on." (laughs) Shit, the kid walked into it that night!

So the fight was on, and almost everybody in the bar crowded into the alley out back. I should mention at this point that I was far from sure that my buddy wouldn't lose the cash he was betting, because Ryan couldn't have weighed more than one-eighty, and I didn't really know if he could fight or not.

Ryan and the black guy squared off with me as the referee, and that big dude just started throwing Ryan all over the place. The kid was getting ragdolled, it was looking bad, and I finally told him,

"Shit, you better do somethin', kid—you better secure the guard!" I know that as the ref I was supposed to be neutral, but I figured I owed Ryan a little advice since he was givin' up about sixty pounds, and layin' on his back in an alley full of glass and rocks! (laughs) Well Ryan did end up securing the guard, and he caught that big dude in an armbar and had 'im squealing like a pig!

I broke it up, and the big dude was PISSED, "That was fucked up, that was bullshit!" But I just said, "You screamed like a bitch and you tapped out, now shut the fuck up and give me that money!" I snatched it out of his hand and gave most of it to my friend, but I also made sure to take a cut for myself, and a bigger cut for Ryan who'd done all the hard work.

We went back inside, and I grabbed a pitcher of Purple Hooter, a vodka/liqueur concoction that I don't know how to make anymore. I put the pitcher and a glass in front of Ryan and got him drinkin', then I grabbed one of the waitresses, brought her over to his table, and said, "You're takin' him home tonight." Sure enough, after her shift was over, she took Ryan home and fucked 'im! She was one of my top-shelf girls, too—I didn't do that for anyone but warriors!

When Phyllis heard about it, she couldn't believe it. She sent me this poor little never-had-a-drink, never-been-fucked kid, and a half-hour later he's gettin' drunk, laid, and fightin' for money in a back alley! (laughs)

She gimme a virgin, and I give her back a hellcat. But that's what you got when you trained with the Iron Bear!

@ironbear95

Chapter Twenty-Six

'SCRAP IRON' ADAM PEARCE

All photos courtesy Adam Pearce.

"The bar-runner goes out to the limo to disperse the group, and then he comes sprinting back and says, 'You HAVE to see this!'"

A standout in the groundbreaking Ring of Honor promotion during its mid-2000s heyday, Pearce is a five-time holder of the National Wrestling Alliance World's Heavyweight Championship—a title previously held by such luminaries as "Nature Boy" Ric Flair, Lou Thesz, Gene "Big Thunder" Kiniski, and Harley Race.

After wrestling all over the globe for nearly 20 years, Pearce retired from the ring in 2014 and accepted a position as a full-time trainer at the world-renowned WWE Performance Center.

The Cove

In early 2000, I was bouncing part-time at a bar in north suburban Chicago called The Cove. Most of the time, the clientele was off-duty Navy and Marines, because Great Lakes Naval Base was pretty close. It wasn't really in a good part of town, so in addition to the military crowd, you'd get your share of run-of-the-mill thugs and thug wannabes. There were usually police cruisers parked right outside the front door, because generally when you get the Navy and the Marines in the same place and you mix in alcohol, a big pissing contest takes place, and you're gonna get at least one fight.

One night, we had more Marines than usual in the bar. They had some kind of early liberty or something, and everybody wanted to get out, get pissed up, and have a good time. Everybody [on the door staff] knew that something was gonna happen on this night.

So we were prepared for that, but what we weren't expecting was for the Navy and Marines to join forces, and get into it with a group of equally drunk wannabe-thug civilians! Thankfully we had a full complement of security, so together with the cops, we managed to get things under control and start removing the guilty parties. It really wasn't anything too bad, except for one situation where three Marines and one Navy dude were beating the shit out of one guy.

We grabbed those [four military] guys and brought them outside, but didn't hand them over to the cops the way we probably would have if they were civilians. We always tried to avoid getting military people arrested. If they were really obnoxious or violent or really fucked up, we'd usually call their commanding officer, and have somebody from the base come and get 'em. We never wanted to have 'em thrown in the [civilian] clink, because that would fuck with their military career and we wanted to take care of those guys.

So we called the commanding officer, and were restraining the [soldiers] and waiting for them to be picked up. They were generally contrite—well, contrite as a drunk can be—until a military van finally pulled up. The commanding officer got out and got the rundown from the head bouncer, and at that point, for no reason that I could see, the Navy guy flipped the fuck out.

He wanted to fight the Marines, he wanted to fight the cops, he wanted fight me and the other bouncers—I mean, some switch just flipped in this dude! His commanding officer started giving him orders, but he just looked at the CO and yelled, "FUCK YOU!" Then he shoved the CO, shoved a cop, took a swing at one of the Marines, took a swing at me—the guy was just a madman! Seeing no alternative, I finally BLASTED the dude right in the chin with as good an elbow as I've ever thrown. I mean, it was SOLID. His head snapped back so far I thought it was going to come off, and after he staggered back against the van, the cops jumped on him and started putting the cuffs on.

They had barely clicked the cuffs shut when out of nowhere, the Navy guy snapped completely out of his daze. I mean WIDE AWAKE, not even selling the elbow one bit, as if it had never happened. With a confused expression on his face, he looked around at everybody and calmly asked, "What's going on? What's happening? Why am I in handcuffs?" At first, I thought it was an act, but the more he talked, the more he seemed like a completely different person from who he'd been a minute before. Soon, I was convinced that he had no idea about anything that had just happened.

When he was told that he'd attacked his CO and the cops, he started crying and begging. He couldn't believe what he'd done.

It was eerie. Unless he was one of the best actors I've ever seen... I don't know if it was battle trauma, or a split personality, or he was on something besides booze, or what.

But as bad as I felt for the guy, the worst part was him showing ZERO effects from that beauty of an elbow I hit him with. I spent the rest of the night feeling like the biggest pussy, and it became a running joke around the bar for the next few weeks.

Not a very funny one, in my opinion.

Pearce with former NWA World's Heavyweight Champion "Nature Boy" Ric Flair

Rookies

After I moved to California, a buddy of mine got me a job in a little bar called Rookies, which is toward the coast in San Diego, in a suburb called Vista. This place was just a dive—I used to call it a "ghetto sports bar." They showed MMA fights in there, as well as this really horrible ghetto-as-you-can-imagine karaoke.

We always had shit going down in there, and it was usually women involved. "You lookin' at my man?" sort of thing. A lot of [racial] conflict in that place—every color of the rainbow was represented, and none of 'em liked each other.

You could rent the place out if you wanted to throw a big party, like a bachelor party. Or local musicians would have record release parties there, where the catering would be chicken wings and Mickey's on tap. You know, bar-food-type shit. I used to always work the front door or the parking lot, because I really just didn't want to be inside that bar.

On one particular night, we're booked for a private party and the place is MOBBED. Including the dance floor, you can legally fit maybe 125 people in there, but I'll bet we have over 200. Me and a couple of other bouncers are at the door, carding people and checking that they're on the guest list. At one point, a limo pulls up and parks in a way that's blocking one of the exits from the parking lot. So we send one of our bar runners over to ask them to move, but the driver tells him, "Just gimme a couple of minutes and then I'll take off." So we give him the time, no problem.

Pretty soon, there's a little crowd of maybe five or six people gathering around the back of the limo, and we send the runner back out there to tell the driver, "Hey, you gotta go already." But the driver's still like, "Hold on, hold on, hold on." So the runner goes to the back of the limo himself, to try to disperse the little group that's staring into the open passenger-side door.

Suddenly, he comes SPRINTING back to where I'm standing and says, "You HAVE to see this!" I go, "Is he going to move the car or what?" but the runner just looks me dead in the eye and says, "GO AND SEE WHAT'S GOING ON."

So I walk out there and work my way through this cluster of dudes who are all hooting and hollering and staring into the limo, and I don't know what to expect. Then, a drunk guy who's standing there, wearing—and I'll never forget this—wearing a white suit and a turquoise shirt with half the buttons open, he looks at me and calmly says, "Dude, you need to just relax and enjoy the entertainment."

He motions toward the open door, and I see three guys, all dressed nice, suits and ties and whatnot, sitting across from this "lady"—make sure you put that word in quotes—who's got her light blue sequined party dress hiked up around her waist, and her knees pulled up to her chest. And she is going to TOWN on herself with a toy! I mean, LIGHT SPEED. At this point, I'm thinking, "What the fuck is goin' on?!" and then Turquoise Shirt Guy gives me this big, sleazy, salacious grin and goes, "Yeeeeeeeeah...!"

I go back to the front door, and the bar runner is laughing HYSTERICALLY. I'm completely at a loss at this point—I mean, what do we do? Tell her to finish up?

Of course, word gets out inside the bar that what's going on in the parking lot is one hell of a lot more entertaining [than the party], so that little group at the back of the limo goes from five, to ten, to twenty. Finally, I get one of the managers to come out and I tell him, "We don't know how to handle this. You wear the collared shirt for a reason, so this one's all you, buddy."

He goes out and views the festivities, and then he talks to one of the guys in the limo and tells him that they have to split. So the limo door finally closes, and the car pulls away.

Just as fast as they *came*, they were gone. Pun intended.

Chapter Twenty-Seven

SAMOA JOE

All photos courtesy Masanori Horie.

> ***"I'm holding this guy against the wall,
> and all of a sudden I smell something burning.
> Then I realize that it's me!"***

Nuufolau Joel Seanoa, aka Samoa Joe, has over the past ten-plus years risen to become one of the biggest stars on the professional wrestling landscape.

After getting an extremely early start to his show business career (he was only 5 when he performed with his father's Polynesian dance troupe at the 1984 Olympics), Joe grew to develop a unique combination of size, agility, a strong technical game, and a great mind for the wrestling business. This array of gifts and skills distinguished him in Japan's ZERO-ONE wrestling organization, and made him the most popular champion in the history of the US-based Ring of Honor promotion.

After spending close to a decade becoming a multiple titleholder in TNA/IMPACT Wrestling, Joe signed a full-time deal with WWE in 2015 and immediately became one of the top stars of its massively-popular NXT program.

Alley Brawl

I started bouncing way before I should have. My first bouncing job I got when I was maybe eighteen, which is totally illegal in California. A football coach got me the gig, and he said, "Keep your mouth shut, and they'll pay you cash under the table." It was at a sports bar that sponsored our team, in Huntington Beach on Beach Blvd. I don't want to say their name and get them in trouble, because I know that the manager who hired me had no idea I was so young.

They put me at the front door, but I thought I might be pushing my luck checking IDs when I shouldn't even have been in that bar in the first place. So I went to some other bouncers who I played football with, and I told them, "You guys work the front, and I'll just work the back door." Now, that was one of the biggest mistakes I could make, because pretty much everything that went down in that place, went down at the back door. But of course, me being eighteen and not knowing any better... actually, seventeen and a half... I'm like, "Oh yeah, I'll take the back door."

So anyways, a couple of hours into the night, two ladies start fighting in the club. Those are the worst fights to break up, because with guys, you can get in there and get physical with them, but with ladies, it's like you're sticking your hand between two rabid cats. You're gonna get scratched, punched, kicked, and you can't do anything back because it's girls.

Me and this other bouncer separate them, and we're walking them out while they're both going crazy. They're screaming at each other over our shoulders, and it's just a big mess. Then the lady my friend is holding breaks out of his arms, comes charging over, and starts trying to get at the other girl over my back. She throws about six punches and manages to hit ME with every single one of them, never even touching the other girl! So I've got this catfight going on literally on top of me as I push them both out the back door.

Finally, we separate 'em and get 'em somewhat calmed down. We're telling them, "You go to your car, you go to your car," when one girl's extremely drunk boyfriend comes storming out of the bathroom, where I guess he was throwing up. He doesn't know the situation, he just sees us dealing with his girlfriend, and of course now he wants to kick everybody's ass. So I'm trying to calm him down, but he's not having it, and then the girls start gearing up to fight again.

I don't want this whole thing kicking off a second time, so while I'm dealing with the dude, I just lean back and stick my arm out, interject it between the two girls, kind of like I'm boxing out for a rebound. But one of the girls was off-balance, and it caused her to fall backward and skin her knee. Terrific. Of course it's immediately all my fault, and she starts calling me this and this and this. And when I try to help her up from the ground, her boyfriend hauls off and coldcocks me from the side! I mean, he just catches me right on the button, one of those deals where I'm starting to go down, my knees are buckling, but then the reset button hits.

I straighten most of the way back up, then grab the guy and rush him into the wall. I got him pinned there, but I'm still feeling that punch and trying to get my head back together. The guy's a bit smaller than me —I'm maybe two-eighty and he's about two-ten—and I'm pressing my forearm up under his chin as hard as I can 'cause I don't wanna get hit again. He's fighting, kicking, you know, and now the girl's on me too from the blindside. Now, I don't know it's a girl at this time, I just know I'm being attacked. The dude's fighting hard, he kicks me in the balls a couple times, and I'm just trying to stay standing. Basically, it's a nightmare scenario. Where the other bouncer's at, I have no idea, but I'm pretty sure he was just sitting there, negotiating with the other chick while I'm getting pummeled by this couple.

Now, kind of your standard bouncer equipment in Cali is your Dickey's work jacket. They're strong, they're durable, and if somebody pulls a knife, they'll protect you a little bit. Not from stabbing, but a little bit from anything slashy. So I've got one of 'em on like everybody else, and that would soon be something I was very thankful for.

I'm still holding this guy against the wall, and all of a sudden I smell something burning—then I realize that it's me! The chick has one of those windproof lighters and she's trying to burn my neck! The thing's up close to my skull and the heat's like a fuckin' laser, but for now there's so much movement going on that she's just burning a hole into the collar of my Dickey's jacket. At this point, I still haven't turned to see that it's a woman—all I know is that I feel heat, I smell smoke, and this girl... if she would have screamed "get off my man" or some shit, I probably wouldn't have done what I did. But she didn't.

I'm half knocked-out, this guy's kicking me in the balls, I'm getting burned in the collar, and I just... I throw a back elbow probably as hard as humanly possible. I look back, and all I see is high heels upside-down at eye level.

I have just turned this lady inside-out with a back elbow.

At that exact time, two buddies of the guy I'm fighting come running out the door, just in time to see me back elbowing the SHIT out of the guy's girlfriend. So here I am—seventeen years old, half-concussed, kicked in the balls, holding one large dude against the wall, and now his two buddies are destined to kick my ass.

I immediately get tackled to the ground, and I look up and see a boot coming down to stomp me, and I'm thinking, "This is it." But out of nowhere, the elderly manager comes out the back door swinging an extendable baton that he kept behind the bar. The next thing I hear is these nice thuds and whacks and guys falling down, and then the manager drags me out of the fray.

Soon the one guy's laid out, the other guy's got a gash in his head and he's cussin' up a storm, the guy I had pressed against the wall is damn near passed out from me leaning on his throat, and then of course there's the knocked-out girl on the ground. I'm lying there, looking all around me and thinking, "Okay, the next thing that happens is the cops are gonna show up, and I'm an illegal seventeen-year-old bouncer who's just beaten up a girl, punched this guy…" For me it was like the end of the world, I didn't know what up.

The other bouncers sit me up against this retaining wall that leads to a bunch of apartments, and then they get to work pulling the bodies out of the road. There's a little bit of "F this, F that" from the awake ones, but it's weak. Nobody wants any more at this point.

I pull off my jacket—which I still own to this day—and there's a huge burn mark where that chick almost got through to my neck.

But I barely have time to register that before I hear sirens, loud and getting louder fast. Sure enough, somebody called the cops. They come screeching around the corner, and all you see next is my big ass jumping up and over a six-foot wall, then running through a bunch of apartments and jogging a mile and a half to get home.

By the next week, I'd decided to quit that job until I was legal enough to do it. I mean, fist fights were one thing, but people trying to burn me was something else. So I gave the boss seven days' notice, and he was totally cool about it.

However, being a sponsor of my football team, he was also at our next game a couple of weeks later. When he saw my name in the program, I'm sure he was shocked to find out that the guy he hired was only seventeen! (laughs)

Joe wearing a kick-ass Roots of Fight shirt while hangin' with pro wrestling superfan Masa Horie.

The Secret Deal

When I returned to bouncing a few years later, I quickly realized that a lot of guys wanna challenge the big guy in the bar. I'm talking about the "tough guys," the guys who are looking to get into it. I realized quick that if you get physical every time a tough guy steps to you, you're gonna be throwing punches all night. So I got real masterful with my shit, and became a master of the passive bouncing technique.

For example, there might be two dudes brawling on the dance floor, and of course they got their posses around. So I'd get in there and push one of the guys against the wall, and right away I'd start feeding shit into his head. "You okay, dude? I saw him sucker punch you, that was fuckin' bullshit!"

Now, whether he actually got sucker punched or not, every guy's gonna say the same thing, "Uh…yeah, bro… he totally suckered me! You see that shit?!"

That "sucker punch" intro was always the key. It got 'em thinking that they'd found a brother who was gonna help 'em fight their fight. They'd calm down right away, and I'd have 'em thinking that these weren't the droids they're looking for.

But I still had to get 'em out the door, so I developed what the other bouncers started calling "The Secret Deal." They could tell when I was workin' it too—any time I started acting overly concerned for a guy who'd been in a fight, the boys at the front would say, "Okay, he's bustin' a Secret Deal."

The Secret Deal was always along the lines of, "Hey listen, man… FUCK that guy. What he did was BULLSHIT. I got that fucker rounded up out back, so if you wanna get his ass, go get your boys and you can roll out there and fuck him up, no big deal." I'd even do the fake conversation on my earpiece with nobody on the other end: "Hold on… hey man, you got him? Cool! Okay, brother, they're holding that fucker for you outside, it's on!"

And they would always, ALWAYS take the bait. If you had a group of guys that you had to kick out and you were outnumbered, The

Secret Deal was the ultimate get-out. Those guys would be chompin' at the bit to remove *themselves* from the club, and I'd be laying it on thick to encourage 'em. I'd even be massaging their shoulders as they walked out, like they were Rocky going to the ring! (laughs) They'd walk right out the back door, and as soon as they did, I'd step back inside, slam the door, and problem fucking solved.

But even at that point, some guys didn't catch on. One guy stood outside for upwards of two hours, waiting for us to bring this guy out for him to beat up. Finally, the waitresses started leaving, the bar backs were walking to their cars, and he was like, "What the fuck, dude, are they gonna bring that guy out or what?" And the girls were like, "We closed an hour ago, asshole! Go home." (laughs)

I can't tell you how many dudes—and I'm talking big, violent motherfuckers—we walked out the back door and just straight locked 'em out. Left 'em sitting there, waiting like idiots. We used to keep count, it became a game to see how many Secret Deals we could successfully cut.

If you could sucker guys out instead of gettin' into rumbles with them, the job was ten times more enjoyable. Fewer bruises, less police trouble, and we all got a good laugh over how stupid they were.

🐦 *@SamoaJoe*

Chapter Twenty-Eight

TAIT FLETCHER

All photos courtesy Tait Fletcher.

"The quickness, the brutality of what happened was just shocking. Drag queens, dude—don't ever underestimate 'em."

One of MMA's true renaissance men, Brazilian jiu-jitsu black belt Tait Fletcher stands as a prime example of how to use the sport of mixed martial arts as a springboard to outside-the-sport success. A former bodyguard with a client list including Adam Sandler, Nelly, and Joe Rogan, Tait is also a second-wave member of New Mexico's legendary Team Jackson/Winkeljohn, and a veteran of *The Ultimate Fighter* reality show's third season.

Today, Tait also hosts the popular *Pirate Life* podcast, co-owns the Caveman Coffee Co. with fellow UFC vet Keith Jardine, and continues a successful career as an actor and stuntman. Tait's film/TV resume includes *The Avengers*, *The Lone Ranger*, and *Thor*, but he is perhaps best-known for his recurring role as the white supremacist Lester in the smash-hit AMC series *Breaking Bad*.

The Paramount

I started working in clubs in Michigan during the early 90s. Working before I was even eighteen, at places like Blondie's, St. Andrew's Hall, Harpos... a bunch of bad-ass, dirty old rock clubs. But I really started making a career of it around '97, after I moved to New Mexico. That's around the same time that I started training in jiu-jitsu, after already doing full-contact stick fights with a group called The Dog Brothers.

The first place I worked at was The Drama Club, which segwayed into The Paramount, which is one of the biggest clubs in the southwest. I ended up running the door there, and I always tried to impart to my dudes that they needed to maintain a balance—be respectful to the clients, but also be about your business. While there's gotta be a real clear line that the customers can't cross, whenever possible you have to be polite about enforcing it. A bouncer can say almost anything to anyone, as long as they say it with deference and respect.

That policy got tested one night when we had a bunch of westside gang-bangers already in the place, and then a group of bikers rolled up with their colors on. There were six or eight of 'em, and I had to stop 'em at the door and tell 'em, "Hey guys, I can't have anyone flying colors in here. Now, I understand whatever turn you guys have to take from here, but this is where I have to stand on this." And it worked out, just like it always did when I came at guys with respect and integrity.

On the other side of the coin, sometimes there would be drunk dudes who'd require me to get more physical with them. Usually it was rich kids, little entitled motherfuckers. I remember one time when I stopped in to check on some of my guys and make sure everything was cool.

When I show up [that night], I'm in a crabby mood because I've got a fight coming up in a week. I'm cutting weight, so I'm hungry and skinny and miserable. Then this young dude in a Porsche pulls into a handicapped spot out front, and starts revving his engine like an asshole. He thinks he's in a Chevelle or something, but instead of making a deep rumble and roar, his engine's just making this whiny, irritating noise while he yells out the window, "THAT'S RIGHT, MOTHERFUCKER! THAT'S RIGHT!" I don't know who he thought he was impressing because there was nobody around, just us standing inside the door.

Of course, I'm immediately thinking that this is not a guy I want in the bar.

The kid gets out of his car and walks up—he's a big kid—and I go, "Hey homie—you can't park there. You'll get towed."

"Fuck that, I can park where I want."

"No dude, that's a handicapped spot, you'll get towed. In fact, you know what dude? You should just bounce. Tonight's not your night —come back and see us another time."

That pisses him off. "Oh yeah? What are you, some kind of ass-kicker? You just going around kicking ass all day, is that it?"

And I'm thinking, "Yes, that's exactly it. Every single day, twice a day, for the last six weeks. Kicking ass is exactly what I've been doing."

Then he takes a couple steps back, hawks up a big one, and spits it right on my legs. "C'mon, motherfucker! C'mon across the street, motherfucker!"

Now, I always preached to my guys about never leaving the door, about always taking the high road and staying safe, but this was the one time that I was gonna go against that. I look at the kid and say, "Okay, let's go. Across the street in that dark parking lot over there." But he doesn't like the sound of that, even though "across the street" was his idea in the first place. He wants to do it right there on the sidewalk, but I tell him, "I can't have this in front of the club. I can't have people seeing what I'm gonna do to you."

Now he's really backpedaling, saying, "Fuck it, I'm just gonna leave." So I tell him he's a punk motherfucker, and I turn around to walk inside, but as soon as I do, he gets brave and starts talking shit again. Finally, I grab him by the back of the neck and drag him across the street to the parking lot, then let him go and say, "What now, dude?"

And now he's all indignant. "Fuck you, man! You don't know who my family is!" He starts claiming his family is Italian mafia, that the Mexican mafia work for them, and all kinds of other shit. He tells me his name, and I kind of recognize it. In fact, I do suspect that his family might actually be running some shit through New Mexico, but at this point I don't care.

I don't have any patience for displays like this. I'm the kind of guy who, if you pull a gun on me, you're gonna have to pull the trigger. I'm not gonna have some tough guy wave a gun in my face and think he's gonna get a result. The result is that I'm gonna take that gun away and beat you with it. Or else you're gonna shoot me, we've got choices. (laughs)

So I tell the kid, "All that's gonna happen is I'm gonna put you to sleep. I'm not even gonna hurt you, I'm just gonna put you to sleep." That gets him threatening to kill my family, kill my mom, stuff like that—and that's it. I walk forward with my head right out there, begging to be punched, and when he takes a swing at it, I duck, get his back, squeeze him out, and drop him.

The problem with putting somebody out, though, is that it's like tasering somebody. [They wake up] back at 100%, and they don't even know what happened. And that's what this kid does, he springs back up thinking that we only just got to the parking lot. "We gonna do something or what?!" (laughs) And so I arm drag him, and get behind him, and put him out again.

This happens SIX TIMES, by which time we've worked our way back to the sidewalk. The kid's slumping to the ground for the last time when Corey, my guy at the club door, comes across the street with a pair of handcuffs. We all kept a pair of cuffs on us, because in New Mexico you can legally use them to citizen-arrest people.

Every previous time he woke up, the kid was all piss and vinegar, breathing fire and talking about killing everyone. But when he wakes up now and feels those handcuffs on his wrists, it's like, "WHOA." Now he's stone-cold sober. "I'm sorry, dude! I was just fucking around!" He even starts crying a little bit when I tell him that the cops are on the way.

One of the cops who shows up is a guy I train jiu-jitsu with, and he comes over and shines his light on the kid's face. Then he looks at me and says, "Tait, what did you do to this kid? He's got no eyebrows!" Now, that's a detail that you're not necessarily going to to notice when you're getting ready to fight, but I check it now and sure enough, no eyebrows. Beats me how the kid got like that—I don't know if he got messed up and watched *Pink Floyd: The Wall* and shaved 'em off or what, but they are totally gone. And now the kid tries to pin that on me—he tells the cop that I scraped them off on the sidewalk! (laughs)

The kid was a clown, but it turned out that his family really was legit connected. So a couple of people went and talked to them on my behalf, making it clear that it was better to just drop the whole thing. Which, thankfully, they did.

Tait with BREAKING BAD co-star Aaron Paul at the series finale wrap party.

Getting 'Em Out

It could get pretty crazy inside The Paramount. Its capacity was six hundred, but sometimes we'd pack eight hundred in there. One night, I got into it with a dude who grabbed a chick he wasn't supposed to grab. I got him in an over/under [clinch], and we were wrestling in this little hallway when a bunch of his pals came at me. One of the guys broke a beer bottle over my head—I couldn't block it with my hands tied up—and I slipped on the beer and broken glass and went down. I was FUCKED. But thankfully, like most people, these dudes weren't educated fighters. I took their buddy's back and used his body as a shield while I choked him to sleep, and without meaning to, they kicked the SHIT out of him trying to get to me! (laughs) Finally, one of my guys showed up and helped me get all of them outta there.

Another time, a guy who was standing by the bar turned around and backhanded his old lady. Now, I know that any broad that's gonna fuck with a dude who's really shitty to her is gonna sign up for that shit every time. You cannot help those people. But at the same time, I had to follow my policy of "Mind your business, but also mind your store."

I went over and turned the guy towards me, and said, "You can't fuckin' do that, dude. Whatever you do in your own home is your own business, but now you gotta bounce." But just as I'm saying that—Ka-DISH!—a bottle breaks over my head, and it was the little bitch who got slapped who swung it! My guys came running over, and we quickly got 'em both outside and handed 'em off to the cops.

Like I said, you cannot help some people.

Gina Storm

Saturday night was a huge gay night. There was one particular drag queen who used to come in named Gina Storm. Gina was a bad motherfucker—she used to be called "Louie" or something. One night, a straight dude came in, one of those dudes who goes to gay clubs because he knows that straight girls go there to relax, and not get harassed by knuckleheads like him.

Gina was in there with a couple of her girlfriends, and this dude looks at her and says something like, "You creepy freak." Of course she got offended, and then he said, "Fuck you, you're a dude and I'll knock you out like one!"

Well, man... that was IT! That was a WRAP! Ooo-WEE! The quickness, the brutality of what happened was just shocking. I was awestruck over how much damage Gina was able to do before I could get over there and stop it.

Drag queens, dude—don't ever underestimate 'em.

Homicidal Hairdresser

Another time, we had this gay hairdresser dude get into an argument with his drag queen girlfriend out in the parking lot, and he went into his car and got a pair of scissors. A bunch of us went out and circled him, and he started swinging those shears at everybody, trying to cut us. Finally, my friend Brendan Casey grabbed his arm as I shot a double [leg takedown], and we got the guy down, took his scissors away, turned him over, and cuffed him.

When the cops showed up, one of them looked at me and said, "This guy is really lucky that he was dealing with you instead of us. If he had been that close to us and threatening us with a weapon, our training dictates that we double-tap him right away. We ask a person to put their weapon down only once, and if they don't comply immediately, we kill them. You probably saved this guy's life."

Twat Cop

Once we had a group of guys step outside the club for a minute, and one of 'em was an off-duty state cop who was a real fuckin' twat. He was a young guy, and I guess he thought he was something special because, in the caste system of cops, the state cops are at the top of the heap, above city cops and sheriffs.

We used to regularly walk through the parking lot to make sure everyone got to their cars safely, and on this occasion I'm out there with some of my guys when the cop fires his gun into the air. No reason, just being a fucking idiot. At first we all duck, and then I finally see who it was [who fired the shots] and he's standing over there, laughing. I straighten up and march right toward him, walking fast, and when he sees me coming, he stops laughing and starts to raise the gun up at me. But by that time, I'm close enough to peel it out of his hand and smash him in the face with it, and then I throw it on the roof of the adjacent courthouse.

You'd think his friends would be on the attack, but instead they immediately started apologizing to me. Not because I'm a tough guy or anything, but just because they wanted to get back into the club. Never mind that their buddy just got his face caved in—these dudes were such parasites that they only cared about kissing my ass, because they knew I was in charge of who got back in.

Unbelievable—that's what kind of a crazy world I was living in.

Moving On

The reason I finally stopped bouncing is that I was getting dark. It's weird when you look at humanity through a bouncer's eyes—you start to see every shift, every situation as an "us or them" scenario. And that's really what it is—you're on a team with five or ten other guys, but if enough dudes come in who are legitimately tough, obnoxious, and trained, they could take over the whole place. Bouncers are almost always outnumbered and outgunned—[what they do is] just a front, a show, a magic trick.

It eventually got to be too much. I was tired of the pressure, tired of seeing people at their worst. I felt like doing that job day after day after day was robbing me of my own humanity. Shortly after [I stopped bouncing], I moved to California to make a go of fighting. I fought for the World Extreme Cagefighting title, fought in the UFC on *The Ultimate Fighter* reality show, started getting into movies, and never looked back.

I'm grateful for what I learned during my time as a bouncer, but I'm also super appreciative that I don't ever have to do that anymore.

🐦 *@TaitFletcher*

🌐 *www.TaitGFletcher.com*

🌐 *www.CavemanCoffeeCo.com*

Chapter Twenty-Nine

PAUL 'TYPHOON' CHENG

Photo courtesy Victor Totten/Heel Hook Photography.

"As they walked past the skanky chick— PAP! PAP! PAP!—bottles came raining down onto that broad's head!"

A former college football standout, British Columbia's six-foot-three, two-hundred-seventy-five-pound Paul "Typhoon" Cheng followed his brief run in the Canadian Football League (CFL) with a cup of coffee in professional boxing before finally settling into mixed martial arts.

After quickly amassing a 3-1 pro MMA record, Cheng signed a six-fight deal with the powerhouse ONE Championship organization as their first Chinese heavyweight fighter. In December 2013, he made his ONE FC debut with a first-round TKO victory over world Muay Thai champion Alain Ngalani.

Van Damme at Gorgomish

I started bouncing in 2000 while I was still in college. I was one of the original guys at a place in Coquitlam called The Foggy Dew. [Grey Cup-winning offensive lineman] Chris Burns was the manager at the time. I bounced around between there and a couple of other places until 2002, when I got drafted in the CFL as a defensive tackle. First round, sixth pick overall. That sounds good, but in hindsight it was kind of a crappy situation, because I ended up stuck behind three ten-year vets, all of them CFL all-stars. I knew that the plan was for me to succeed them, but I couldn't handle it. I didn't have the patience to wait for them to start dying off. I kept thinking, "I was a star in college! Why am I sitting on the bench?" So I played only seven games, and ended up being a first-round bust. It was pathetic.

After that, I returned to bouncing, and ended up at an after-hours place in downtown Vancouver called Gorgomish.

One night, just as the sun was coming up and I was close to the end of my shift, I scanned the room and saw a guy who looked familiar. I looked a little closer and yup, it was Jean-Claude Van Damme, and he was FUCKED out of his mind! You could see with a single glance that he was all wired out of his face, and he came up and asked me if I could find somebody who could hook him up with some... whatever, you know. It wasn't a surprise because I'd heard a lot of things about him being into that kind of stuff, but I ain't anybody's dealer so I told him he had to find it on his own.

A few minutes later, he waved at me and motioned for me to come into the bathroom with him. I thought he was calling me over because there was a problem in there, but when I followed him in, I could see that he found what he was looking for and was inviting me to do some. I politely told him no, and then he started getting really weird—like, all touchy-feely—and I'm thinking, "I gotta get the fuck out of here."

For the rest of my shift, he was chasing me around the place and trying to give me his number. He kept looking me up and down and saying, "We need to do *Bloodsport 2*! You can be the bad guy, you make Bolo [Yeung] look like a little child!" I was just laughing, you know? Thinking, "This guy's too fucked up, I gotta get the fuck away from him." I'd heard a lot of stories about him and squirrels up his ass or whatever, so I was like, "See you later." The last thing I needed was to wake up in a hotel room with this guy doing whatever he might be into!

Corey Feldman

On another night at Gorg, a friend of mine comes in with Corey Feldman, who's in town doing a reality show with Corey Haim. My friend asks me to keep an eye on Feldman and his wife for a while, and right away I can see that the guy is a total space cadet. He's so fucked up and paranoid, when he goes to the restroom he starts saying, "I have to be alone in here! I have to be alone!" So I'm like, "Okay, fuck" and I gotta go around to everyone and ask them to give us five minutes.

He goes into one of the stalls for a while, and when he comes back out he's even spacier. I was only too happy to hand him back over to my friend at the end of the night. Later on somebody told me that Feldman was doing tons of K [ketamine], which would certainly explain the way he was acting.

Daddy-O's

Later, I moved on to a really rough place called Daddy-O's. One night, there was this dirty, dirty little white girl sitting up on one of the dance risers with her miniskirt hiked up, just sitting there and playing with her box in front of everybody. It wasn't a pretty sight— in fact it was fucking disgusting, because on a scale of one to ten, she was MAYBE a drunk six. Like, if you had ten beer you might say, "I'll just take it home and deal with it." A ten-beer kind of situation.

Then I saw this group of hot little Asian girls. I didn't even see where they came from, suddenly they just appeared, walking across the dance floor. And as they walked past the skanky chick—PAP! PAP! PAP!—five or six bottles came raining down onto that broad's head! And then chairs! Normally, you'd think [the Asian chicks would yell], "Oh, you skank" and stuff like that, but these girls didn't say nothing, they just went straight to massacring that chick!

The skank had blood all running down her face, and I was scrambling around trying to chase the Asian chicks away, but it was like trying to control a bunch of cats. I mean, what are you supposed to do? With guys, you can just clock 'em, but girls... you stop 'em, take their bottle away and say, "Stay here!" and they just go, "NO!" and run off to get another one.

The slutty chick's face was a mess, cut wide open, and I wanted to help her, but you know, I also didn't want to touch the blood of a dirty-ass skank who's been showing her box all over the place. Me and the other bouncers managed to hold off the Asian chicks until the ambulance arrived, and I think the skank ended up being okay. But I was paranoid for a month about how maybe that dirty chick's blood might have splashed on me.

Calling It Quits

I'm happy to have all that stuff behind me, because that scene wasn't taking me anywhere. Now that I'm away from all the partying and the bar fights, I'm able to put my full attention toward my MMA career. But I did get something positive out of my time as a bouncer, because just like I don't feel any pressure fighting in front of a crowd after playing football in front of fifty thousand people, I'm sure as hell not scared of my opponents in the cage after all those times I could have got shot, stabbed, or wolf-packed.

After all those years of bouncing, MMA is something I had no trouble adapting to.

🐦 *@TyphoonCheng*

Chapter Thirty

MONIQUE GANDERTON

All photos courtesy Monique Ganderton.

"It looked like both girls were going to walk away, but then they started going after each other like enraged hamsters!"

An accomplished equestrian, snowboarder, gymnast, skater, diver and track athlete, Monique "Mo" Ganderton has as diverse a resume as anyone you'll find in this book.

Not content with making pouty faces in her career as a professional model, Monique was inspired by a chance meeting with Sylvester Stallone to carve a niche for herself in show business. Nearly a decade and a half later, she has appeared in numerous blockbusters including *I Robot*, *Watchmen*, *The Wolverine*, *Iron Man 3* and two installments of *The Hunger Games* series.

A talented actor in her own right and a stunt double for some of Hollywood's biggest stars, including Sigourney Weaver, Famke Janssen, and Nicole Kidman, Monique is a performer for whom I can personally vouch as being not only talented and tough, but also as cool as balls.

The Phoenix

Back in the day, I was doing background work on movies in Toronto while trying to get into stunts, and one day I met this massive ex-football player who was also doing background. He ran security at a club called The Phoenix, and he said, "We need a girl, come be a bouncer."

Now, I hate bartending, because I don't want to wear the push-up bra and sleazy outfit and have to be nice to frickin' drunk dudes, so bouncing sounded like a MUCH better job for me. But I had no idea about bouncing in general or this place in particular, and I definitely didn't know what I was getting into!

Violence-wise, I'd already seen a lot of crazy stuff in [my hometown of] Edmonton. Machete fights, bouncers throwing guys through windows—this was just the stuff you saw at a normal bar. One time, a guy got stabbed really bad while trying to break up a fight, and he ran out of the club with his guts literally in his hands. I have never once gone down Whyte Avenue on a weekend night without seeing a fist fight.

But even with all that, Toronto still had some surprises for me.

Working The Door

The Phoenix was in a pretty gnarly East Toronto neighborhood that was full of strip clubs and stuff, and it was known for having the city's biggest hip-hop night. So there I was, this skinny, punk-rock white girl working in the roughest part of town with ten of the biggest, blackest ex-football player bouncers you ever saw! (laughs) Our clientele included every kind of gangster, prostitute, stripper, and drug dealer that you could imagine—I always felt like our club attracted all the people who couldn't get into the other hip-hop nights. (laughs) On other days, The Phoenix would have metal shows and punk shows as well, but Sunday, our hip-hop night, was the roughest night for sure.

One of my duties was checking IDs and purses at the door. It was common for me to ask a drunk girl to empty out her pockets, and have her pull out a huge bag of cocaine. I'm like, "Okay, I'll just take that and turn it in, thanks!" We must have confiscated every kind of drug imaginable, but especially cocaine, this was a cocaine type of place. We didn't usually call the cops for that, or for much else, really—only for really bad fights. If you called the cops every time you found a weapon, or a bag of coke or weed, the cops would just have to stay there all night. So I turned in all the drugs I found to the boss, and I didn't know, or want to know, what happened to them from there! (laughs)

I learned so much about drugs working at that place, as well as about how much bizarre shit chicks carry in their purses. I'd be searching a purse and it would be like, "Really? You have roller skates, a curling iron, a full change of clothes…" It was ridiculous, those chicks were nuts. I never found guns on any of the girls, but once in a while, a guy would try to sneak one in. [Guys mainly carried] knives though, and they were so common that when a guy got

L.   Mo lookin' HAWT in HANSEL & GRETEL: WITCH HUNTERS.

R.   Mo with fellow stunt performer/main squeeze Sam Hargrave in
     CONAN THE BARBARIAN.

caught with one, he'd usually just say, "Oh, I forgot about that" and
then go get rid of it before coming back for a patdown.

I learned a lot about fake IDs, too. It was very common for a
young girl to come up with a fake, out-of-town ID in the hope of
confusing me. She'd be like, "Here's a Michigan ID," but since those
were popular ones to counterfeit, I had found out what the real ones
looked like. One night, a girl showed up with an Alberta license that
was pink and all these other colors, and she said, "It's brand new,
they just came out with it." You should have seen her face when
I pulled out MY Alberta license and said, "That's funny, it looks
nothing like this!" (laughs)

We had a pimp who used to come in every Sunday with his girls, and half of them would have those pink Michigan or Alberta licenses. I'd just be like, "Sorry, I can't take this, and I hope that you don't have to sit outside and wait because it's effing cold." That was actually kind of scary, because you only have to be nineteen to get into a bar in Toronto, so I'd be looking at these working girls and thinking, "How old *are* you?"

Racism

Growing up in Edmonton, I didn't really get to experience black culture, so it was cool hanging out with the [other bouncers] and listening to their stories and stuff. Being around those guys really opened my eyes to how much racist, disturbing shit they had to deal with from gnarly, drunk patrons.

One night, a white guy got kicked out and he was super pissed-off about it, so he just started dropping N-bombs all over the place. I looked back at my co-workers—who were usually the sweetest guys ever—and all ten of them were taking out their earplugs and putting their radios on the ground. One of them said, "Mo, this is your other job, picking up our walkies," and then they took off after the white guy who had realized what was happening and bolted. That left me standing all by myself at the front door, with walkies all over the ground around me! (laughs)

Finally the guys came back, and I was almost scared to ask what happened to the white dude. But they told me that they'd gone easy on him—just tackled him, held him down, and scared the shit out of him for a while. Let him know that it wasn't cool to say shit like that.

It would shock you how many people used to say racist shit to those guys on a daily basis.

The "Ladies" Room

Aside from breaking up and preventing fights—and picking up walkies (laughs)—my job was [supervising] the women's bathroom. That involved a lot of disgusting stuff, like picking up a drunk chick who's splayed over the toilet wearing nothing but a tank top dress. Head in a pile of vomit, cooch out, just NASTY. The guys would always laugh at me when shit like that happened, "Okay Mo, you handle this one—that's the GIRL'S room, we can't go in there!" (laughs) They would just be loving it, they thought it was so funny.

A lot of the stuff I saw in there was just gross, like people having sex in a barf-covered toilet stall. I don't understand people having sex in clubs anyways, but especially not in there! And drugs—I caught a LOT of people doing drugs. I kept thinking, "If these people were able to get their drugs in here, somebody's not doing their job out front—and that somebody's probably me!" (laughs) Not on purpose, but I definitely let a few things slip through the cracks.

I did have to break up one fight in the washroom and it scared the shit out of me. It's one thing when dudes fight, there's usually a lot of puffing up and stuff, but when girls fight, it goes straight from being totally calm and, "Oh no, it's cool", to "RAAAAWR!!!" Full-on!

It was weird because when I first showed up, it looked like both girls were going to walk away and let it go. But then one of them gave the other a disrespectful little tap, and just like that they were going after each other like enraged hamsters! Luckily I'm pretty tall, so I was able to hold the girls at arm's length and call for help, the whole time thinking, "Please do not scratch me in the eyeball!" (laughs)

After we got them out, there was a trail of press-on nails and pieces of weave all the way from the bathroom to the door. Just BRUTAL.

🐦 *@MoGanderton*

ⓦ *www.MoniqueGanderton.com*

Chapter Thirty-One

DARREN SHAHLAVI

Photo courtesy Loyd Bateman.

"Two of my guys started unscrewing various items from the walls—baseball bats, ski poles, basically anything that could be used as a weapon."

I could get carpal tunnel typing out all the cool roles that UK-born actor/stuntman/martial artist Darren Shahlavi played prior to his untimely passing in 2015 from an undiagnosed heart condition. You may remember him tangling with Michael Jai White in *Mortal Kombat: Legacy* and *Tactical Force*, trading blows with Donnie Yen and Sammo Hung in *Ip Man 2*, cage fighting with Ty Olsson in *Borealis* (aka *Survival Code*), boxing with Eddie Murphy in *I Spy*, or battling the legendary Stone Cold Steve Austin (and me) in *The Package*.

Fondly remembered for his acting skills, insane martial arts ability, ridiculous physical development and warm, engaging personality, Darren remains a favorite of action movie fans the world over.

Signal Eight

I was twenty years old when I moved to Hong Kong, and twenty-one when I started working for a company called Signal Eight Security. "Signal Eight" is actually the highest typhoon warning level, so I guess they thought it made a cool name for their company.

They started me off doing door work, but I ended up also bodyguarding for visiting celebrities. Signal Eight had some big contracts, they even handled the opening of the Hong Kong Planet Hollywood, so it was no surprise that we got the job to protect Bruce Willis when he scheduled a Planet Hollywood appearance to promote *Die Hard with a Vengeance*.

[The security team] was me and three other guys, but Bruce also arrived with his regular, full-time bodyguard, a giant Israeli guy. When Bruce turned up, he immediately got behind the bar and started serving drinks—he used to be a bartender—and overall, it was looking like it was going to be a fun evening. Then Bruce McLaren, the co-owner of Signal Eight, came up to me and said he'd heard that Jackie Chan might turn up. I thought, "fucking awesome," because I hadn't met Jackie at that time. A while later, I saw Raymond Chow walk in—he's the man who owns Golden Harvest Pictures, the company that produced all the Bruce Lee movies—and I knew that meant Jackie wasn't far behind.

Jackie finally showed up wearing a bright pink track suit. He jumped over the bar and began smiling, waving, shaking hands—

you know, working the crowd. All night long, I found him to be a really nice, polite guy. After a while they did a press conference, showed the trailer for Bruce's movie and talked with Bruce and Jackie about both of their new movies. Then, since it was Bruce's brother David's birthday, they all went into the back room to celebrate while I stayed out in front. And then, as if all that hadn't been enough, Cindy Crawford showed up and went into the back as well!

One of the guys I was working with looked at me and said, "This is awesome! Bruce Willis, Cindy Crawford and Jackie Chan, all here in the bar!" But after I popped out the front door to have a look around, I realized that this was NOT awesome. We had drawn a massive crowd that completely filled up the front of the club and the street outside, and with all three of our celebrity guests almost due to go to a nearby restaurant for dinner, we had to figure out a way to get them through the crowd to their cars.

We ended up recruiting most of the wait staff to form two parallel human chains, making a kind of aisleway through the middle of the crowd. It worked like a charm. Getting Bruce out was actually pretty easy, because I guess the Hong Kong fans bought into his tough-guy character, and nobody wanted to risk stepping out of line with him. He got into a limo with his guy, then Cindy Crawford was escorted to her limo by the other two fellows from Signal Eight, and then I got ready to get Jackie out of there. But as I looked out into the street, I didn't see his ride, so I said, "Jackie, where's your car?" He just smiled and said, "Never mind! We can walking! No p'oblem—we can walking!" (laughs) He just didn't give a shit!

Fuckin' hell. Now I had to escort him and Raymond Chow several blocks to the restaurant on foot, with no reinforcements, and Jackie wearing a bloody pink track suit! I thought it would take us hours, and that it would be a nightmare trying to keep people off him, but

Jackie knew how to work a crowd like no one I've ever seen. Smiling, high-fiving, saying hello, but never standing still, always moving. He must have known that if he stopped walking for a second, he'd never get started again.

Surprisingly, the walk took us only ten minutes—we actually arrived before Cindy Crawford did—but I'll tell you, it was ten of the most tense minutes of my life. Every second I was wondering what I would do if the crowd decided to swarm!

Patrick Stewart

I also did security for Patrick Stewart, and his main request beforehand was that he wanted me to wear a suit. He didn't want someone who looked like a bodyguard. I think that with a lot of celebrities, their bodyguards like to play the role and get very close when there

Darren and Donnie Yen between takes in IP MAN 2. Photo courtesy Darren Shahlavi.

are photographers around, because they want to be in the pictures. I know that [Jean-Claude] Van Damme in particular doesn't like that —he thinks it looks cheap—and Stewart didn't like it either. So I learned to step back, to give him his space when the cameras came out. I was with him for five days and he was the coolest guy. Very nice with absolutely everybody, a real gentleman like you'd think he would be.

China Jump

Signal Eight eventually sent me to run the door at this club called China Jump, which was a sports-themed restaurant during the day that turned into a kind of lively bar in the evening. They'd been having trouble with some of the locals—not local Chinese, but Australians, Americans, Canadians and the like who lived there and would occasionally get a bit too rowdy.

I went in there on my first night with another new guy, an American from Philadelphia, who would end up quitting at the end of that first shift. The club had a very high turnover rate—security personnel were always quitting because it would get so crazy.

I had barely started my first shift when two Chinese gentlemen came to the front door, and one of them flashed a two-fingered "peace" sign, but with the back of his hand facing me. Now, I'm from England, where that's the sign for "fuck off," so straight away I was thinking I was into some trouble. I said, "I'm sorry, do you gentlemen have a problem?" but he just did it again! I was starting to really get pissed off when he finally said, "Two people, please." He just wanted to get him and his friend into the club! (laughs)

Later on, it did get crazy when a bunch of the locals I'd been warned about came in. They were all Australian rugby players, really big guys, and I thought, "Fuckin' hell, how am I gonna deal with these guys?" I thought about it for a while, and realized that if this was their favorite club and they were going to be coming in all the time, I had to find a way to get them on my side. Not just so that I wouldn't have problems with them, but also so I'd have backup if anything happened with other customers.

So I went over to them, introduced myself as the new doorman, and bought them all a round of drinks. That got us off on the right foot, and the next week when they showed up, I let them in without cover charge and bought them another round. From then on, I made sure that they never had to pay admission, and eventually I became very close with them. It got to the point that whenever a situation came up, one of them would say, "We've got trouble, mate." Not "you've" got trouble—"we." They were always counting themselves in, and whenever I walked into a situation, there would be at least three or four of them right behind me. That arrangement saved me one hell of a lot of trouble on more than a few occasions!

One Friday, one of our guys named Winston threw out a couple of Indian fellas, and they threatened to send people to come back and chop us all up. At the time, we thought it was just tough talk, but the very next night—which was supposed to be my night off—I got a phone call saying, "You'd better get down here quick, and bring as many people as you can."

When I arrived, I asked one of my guys what the problem was, and he said, "Looks like those guys that Winston threw out really meant what they said." He gestured toward a table where four mainland Chinese guys were sitting—I knew they were mainland and not locals because I could hear them speaking Mandarin instead of Cantonese. They were all wearing long coats in the middle of a very hot summer, which immediately got me thinking, "Great, these guys are packing machetes, or worse."

It was an especially tough situation because China Jump was on the seventh floor. You got there from the street by elevator, so there was really no access control. Anyone could just come in off the street, and we didn't see them until they were already in.

I immediately told my guys to get Winston out of sight, and began trying to figure out what I was going to do. While I was racking my brain, two of my guys came out of the manager's office with screwdrivers in their hands, and started unscrewing various items from the walls—baseball bats, skis, ski poles, basically anything that could be used as a weapon. When I saw a guy unscrewing a tennis racquet, I thought, "Okay, this is ridiculous!" (laughs) Then one of my guys came over and turned up the collar of the leather biker jacket I was wearing, making a chopping motion with his hand at the side of my neck and saying, "Just in case."

Fuckin' hell.

I could sense a massacre about to happen, but I knew there had to be an intelligent solution. Finally, I noticed one of our waitresses taking a photograph of a couple that was having dinner, and the bright light switched on over my head. I knew what I was going to do.

I went over and asked the couple if I could borrow their camera, and then I brought the waitress to the table with the four mainland guys and said, "Hey guys, I'm taking pictures with all our happy customers to put up on our wall—do you mind?" Before they could refuse, I posed beside them with a big, beaming grin while the waitress snapped away. "Couple more, couple more—make sure you get everybody in. Smile, guys!" Then I thanked them, and told them that the next time they came in, they should be sure to look for their photos on the wall. I walked away thinking, "God, I fucking hope this works!"

A couple of minutes later, they finished their drinks, put their heads down, and walked straight into the elevator. As soon as I saw that they were on the ground floor, I went straight to the bar and said, "Double vodka—PLEASE!" (laughs)

That was a big relief for us, but from the looks on the guys' faces as they walked out, I honestly think it was also a relief for them. Putting them on camera like that gave them an excuse to get out of doing what they'd been sent there to do, and I think they were happy for that.

Thankfully, we never saw them again, and nothing further ever came out of that situation.

Chapter Thirty-Two

'THE DEAN OF MEAN'
KEITH JARDINE

Photo courtesy Tait Fletcher.

*"I saw three guys in the car ahead of me.
One of 'em was rustling around in the glove box,
so now I'm pretty sure they have a gun."*

Miner, firefighter, bounty hunter, and professional boxer/mixed martial artist—"The Dean of Mean" Keith Jardine has some of the manliest credentials in the history of manliness.

After making his pro MMA debut in 2001, Jardine suffered only one loss in his first thirteen fights, and gained a coveted spot on The

Ultimate Fighter reality show's second season. He parlayed his success on the show into a major league career that included victories over Hall of Fame champions Forest Griffin and "Iceman" Chuck Liddell.

Currently, Jardine focuses on his new careers as an actor/stuntman and co-owner of the Caveman Coffee Co. with his friend and fellow actor/UFC vet Tait Fletcher.

> *Mauler's Note: I'm particularly fond of Keith's stories because they show how bouncing is a job that sometimes follows you home.*

La Casita

Right up until I did the [Ultimate Fighter] reality show, I supported my fighting career by working two jobs—personal trainer during the day and bouncer at night.

One of the hardest places I ever bounced was Las Vegas—not the one in Nevada, but a real small town by the same name in San Miguel county, up in northern New Mexico. Back in the wild west days, it was known as one of the wildest towns of all the wild west towns. For example, they had the highest murder rate, and they used to lynch people in the middle of the park all the time. They had a windmill there that was actually called "The Las Vegas Hanging Windmill," and the townspeople would drag criminals out of the jail and string 'em up on it. Las Vegas had a fighting history, too. In 1912, Jack Johnson knocked out Jim Flynn in a world heavyweight title defense there. I went to college there, and let's just say that the energy from those wild west days never really left. It was still there with the local people, so you had to be pretty careful.

I worked in La Casita, one of the bars that all the local people went to, and every minute of every shift you were always waiting for the big fight to happen. One night, I noticed a guy picking a fight with the bar manager, so I got hold of him and started taking him out. He was so much of a problem that when we finally got to the door, I think I set a new distance record for how far I threw him. After he landed, he picked himself up and started talking about stabbing me and so on, but he didn't do anything and eventually he left.

A week or two later, I was driving down the street when a couple of guys behind me in a big truck started really harassing me, driving aggressive right on my ass. I pulled over to let them pass, but after they went by, something came over me and I thought, "Naw, to heck with that." So I started chasing them, and when they realized that I was on their tail, they slammed on the brakes and I slid right up into 'em, smashed up the whole front of my car.

I started getting out of the car, and saw the driver of the truck walking towards me, and that's when I noticed that it was the same guy I'd thrown out of the bar! Before I could get all the way out, he was on me, reaching over my open door to punch me in the head, and I'm thinking, "Okay, what just happened?"

Naturally, I didn't take kindly to that, and I started fighting back. Drove him all the way across the street until he finally fell down. I hit him a few more times on the ground, but in the back of my mind I was thinking, "His friend's gotta be coming up on me." So I stood up and turned around, and sure enough, the buddy was standing there with a knife in his hand!

By this time, I was winded, man, from going all-out, but I didn't show it. I held my hands up, like, "What?" and we just stood there, staring for a minute, until finally the buddy decided to just grab the

Me and Keith on the set of TACTICAL FORCE.

guy I'd beaten up and go. I'll always consider that one of my better stories, because it didn't get nearly as bad as it could have!

Off-The-Clock Danger

In a small town like that, when you throw people out [of a bar], they know who you are and they watch out for you, so there's no escaping anything. One night, I was headed to my friend's house in my Ford Ranger, and I didn't realize that I had people following me. When I pulled up to the house, they pulled over right in front of me and blocked my vehicle. I was halfway out of my car when I saw three guys in the car ahead of me. One of 'em was rustling around in the glove box, so now I'm pretty sure they have a gun.

I reached behind me, pulled down the back seat and grabbed onto the baseball bat I kept there, hoping the whole time that those guys would think I was grabbing for a gun. And they must have, because after they looked back and saw me rustling around while keeping the bat low and out of sight, they decided to just start their car up and drive off. Not a violent story, but a great one to me because it didn't turn into a disaster.

Talking Tough

Generally, I don't really brag about my time as a bouncer because I don't think there's much to brag about. A lot of bouncers boast about throwing people out of bars, "Yeah, I knocked that guy out, I threw this guy out," but that stuff always annoyed me. To me, knocking drunk people out when you're sober is almost like child abuse. Any sober person should be able to take care of any two drunk people, so knocking out a drunk guy, even when it's necessary, isn't really something to be proud of.

@KeithJardine205

www.KeithJardine.net

www.CavemanCoffeeCo.com

Chapter Thirty-Three

'RAGIN' KAJAN JOHNSON

All photos courtesy Kajan Johnson.

"Every time she started freaking out, I would squeeze my legs and cut off the blood to her brain."

After making his MMA debut at the age of seventeen, rapper/ fighter "Ragin" Kajan Johnson battled thirteen times in twenty-one months against anyone who was willing to stand across the ring or cage from him.

After losing a hard-fought battle to current Team Tristar stable-mate Rory MacDonald in 2007, Johnson went on a tear, losing only once in his next nine fights while garnering the XMMA lightweight championship and gaining a coveted spot on *The Ultimate Fighter* reality show.

In May 2015 he finally notched his first official Ultimate Fighting Championship victory, over 13 years after his entry into professional MMA.

Fyre

Right before I moved to Montreal to join Team Tristar, I bounced on Vancouver's Granville Street strip at a place called Joseph Richard. To be honest, not much crazy shit happened there. I mean, I knocked a guy out with a head kick one night, but nothing really crazy. But up north in my hometown of Prince George—now, that was a different story.

When this story happened, I was already fighting [professionally], and also bouncing at a place called Fyre. One night a bunch of my friends came in, guys who were both MMA fighters and legitimate thugs. I was previously in the thug life myself, and even though I had gotten out of it, those guys were still my boys.

At the same time that they were in the club, there was a big wedding party in the upstairs VIP area. About forty out-of-towners from nearby Kelowna, and few of them were also MMA fighters. You get that far north and you'll find a ton of fighters, because there's not much to do except drink, fight, and fuck.

My then-girlfriend Rochelle was the only server working that night, and she was going up and down the stairs, serving both levels. But after they'd gotten a few drinks into them, the guys in the wedding party started doing creepy stuff toward Rochelle. She's smoking hot, so c'mon, of course guys are going to hit on her. Es-

Kajan (right) with former adversary, now friend and stablemate Rory MacDonald.

pecially in a town like Prince George, which is absolutely NOT known for hot chicks to the point that people would look at Rochelle and go, "What is she even doing here?"

Eventually though, one of the guys went a little too far and put his hands on her, so I went up there and issued a warning. The guy took it well enough, he promised to be respectful and not do it again, so it was all good. Or so I thought.

But word about what happened trickled through the bar staff, and then it got around to my thug friends. And one of my friends, a guy named Tyler Borrowman, who was not just an MMA guy and not just a thug, but also completely batshit crazy, he went upstairs and all fucking hell broke loose.

Within seconds, we had sixty people just BRAWLING, and I'm talking about people who really KNOW how to fight! The whole wedding party was wearing suits, and my friends were all thugged up, so it was like two armies with different uniforms and everybody was just SCRAPPING.

I knew that if I let Tyler do what he wanted, he was gonna end somebody's life, so I ran up there and started chasing him all over the place. Pulling him off one person and unintentionally throwing him onto another, then pulling him off that guy, and so on. I didn't even pay attention to the rest of the giant melee—my whole job was just centered on keeping Tyler from murdering people! (laughs)

When the cops finally started coming in the front door, we hustled all my friends out the back so that the only people that ended up getting hauled off were from the wedding party. Which as far as I was concerned, meant a good night all around! (laughs)

Scrappin' With The Amazon

A few months later, in the middle of winter, we had trouble with this big, tall, amazon kind of girl, and when we told her she had to go, she went completely insane. It ended up with me holding her arms and upper torso, another guy holding her legs, and a third guy holding the door while she fought us with everything she had. Her boyfriend was in the club too, but he just stayed put and let us carry his crazy bitch away! (laughs)

We took her outside and put her down in the middle of the street, and she started yelling about how we "violated" her because her skirt had rode up, and well, things were showing. But hey, that wasn't our fault—you don't want your stuff showing, don't act a fool in a skirt!

When she got up off the pavement, she was looking for REVENGE. She ran at us, attacked us, and that's when I hit my limit. This chick had to get dealt with. But of course, you can't punch a girl, so instead I armdragged her, took her down, and pinned her to the ground. But this chick was strong, crazy, and First Nations—which is a really dangerous combination—so I stepped over into the full mount [straddling her chest] and got as much of my weight on her as possible. That just made her even crazier—kicking, scratching, ripping my clothes—so I pushed her hand down, wrapped my leg around the back of her neck, and put her in a mounted triangle choke! (laughs)

Now remember, this is winter in Prince George—it's like, MINUS THIRTY-FIVE—and we're in the middle of the street with me mounted on top of her! But she STILL wouldn't settle down—in fact, she was bucking and thrashing so much that we ended up back on the sidewalk! I'll tell you, it was some serious rodeo shit—I should have got a prize for staying on top for more than eight seconds.

The only thing that saved me was that every time she'd start freaking out, I would squeeze my legs and cut off the blood to her brain. That would calm her down until I relaxed and let the blood come back to her head, and then she'd start freaking out again. So I just kept turning her off, letting her wake up, and turning her off again. (laughs) It was completely fucking insane!

Eventually, the cops drove up, and you can imagine what it looked like to them. When they got out of the car, I said, "I've got her triangled, but when I let her go, she's gonna freak out so you guys better be ready." But thankfully, she decided it wasn't a good idea to freak out at cops, so she did what they told her to do and the whole thing finally settled down.

Only in Prince George, man! (laughs)

 @iamragin

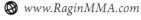 www.RaginMMA.com

Chapter Thirty-Four

'EL GUAPO' BAS RUTTEN

Photo courtesy Bas Rutten.

"We're walking in, and I have a gun hidden. All the people know us and they're like, 'Okay, bad shit is gonna happen now.'"

If there existed an International Bouncers' Hall of Fame, it would have an entire wing named after UFC Hall-of-Famer "El Guapo" Bas Rutten, as well as a statue of his likeness out front. Why, you may ask? Because Bas Rutten is quite simply the greatest bouncer of all time.

Now, Bas is one of my closest friends, so of course I'm biased, but I'm also far from being the only one with that opinion. During their own interviews, many of this book's other subjects asked me, "You're getting Bas for this, right? You've gotta get Bas."

As a former Dutch Muay Thai champion, karate and tae kwon do black belt, undefeated King of Pancrase, and UFC heavyweight champion, Bas Rutten is one of those rare individuals who was simply created to mess people up.

During his world-beating heyday, Rutten's superhero-esque physical abilities, primal instincts, and considerable intellect were focused exclusively on the task of dominating his opponents in ways ranging from the slickly technical to the horrifyingly brutal. Not bad for a guy who started out as a badly-bullied child, so crippled by asthma that he'd be confined to his bed for weeks at a time.

It says a lot about Rutten that he has always contrasted his lethal performances with a gregarious and charismatic personality, which in recent years has turned him into a film and TV star, an internationally sought-after commentator, and an idol to legions of adoring fans.

But before all the bright lights, world titles, and red carpets, Bas Rutten forged a savage legend in the clubs, streets, and alleyways of his native Netherlands that endures to the present day.

And so, with extreme pride and pleasure, WHEN WE WERE BOUNCERS presents these exclusive stories of El Guapo's early days.

Ladies and gentlemen—Bas Rutten.

The Galaxy

For a while, I worked at a bar called The Galaxy, a bad-ass bar that was very well-known in Holland, in a town called 's-Hertogenbosch.

We had two or three bouncers downstairs, and upstairs, three more bouncers. When the criminals came in, they had to give their guns to us. We would hide them, store them like a coat check! (laughs)

When you go into the club, there was a door for the regular customers that leads downstairs. To go upstairs to the VIP club, you go a different way up this big staircase, and halfway up the stairs you have to pay. You need a stamp after you pay, because we would have 2500 people inside the club, and we need to know who did and didn't pay for the upstairs.

So I am working on the stairs, and this guy walks up, a big, roided guy, and he wants to be all cool. He says, "I don't need a stamp. You know me." I say, "Actually I've never seen you in my life, just let me give you a stamp on the inside of your wrist where it won't show." But he refuses the stamp, and gives me kind of an attitude as he pays, so after he goes inside I remember this.

A while later, he goes downstairs, and then he comes back up with two chicks, one on one arm and one on the other arm. So I stop him and I say, "Can I see your stamp?" (laughs) Of course I remember him, I just say this because he's an asshole. He gets real close and says, "You know me!" and I say, "No I don't, and you have to pay admission."

A young Bas showing off his first Muay Thai title belt. Photo courtesy Bas Rutten.

So he looks at his chicks and says, "Excuse me, ladies, I got a problem to take care of," and then he quickly head butts me in the face! I totally didn't expect it because he was still holding onto the chicks, and he caught me good but I wasn't hurt. So I right away grab him by the shoulders, and I drop two head butts back—BOOM, BOOM—and he goes falling down the stairs. As he's rolling to the bottom, I'm yelling to all the other bouncers, "DID YOU SEE THAT?! DID YOU SEE THAT?!" because it was awesome how he gives me one, and I give him two back! (laughs) Coolest thing ever.

Stupid guy, he didn't think about how he couldn't put any power behind his head butt because he was holding onto the chicks. He nailed me, and it was unexpected, but it was impossible for him [to hurt me]. He probably thought I was gonna be scared after the head butt, but well, it didn't happen like that. (laughs)

Theo

In Holland, when you have to go to court, that means you really fucked it up and you went too hard.

One time, at a company Christmas party, a week before I was [scheduled to fight] in a Thai boxing match, this middle-aged guy goes crazy. He hits a woman, then he hits a guy, then he hits my mother-in-law! He has like, delirium, and he is foaming around his mouth and freaking out.

Even though I am just a guest and not a bouncer at this place, I still have to do something. So I grab him from the back and say, "You gotta stop this, bud—we will go outside and I'll find you a tree, and you can hit the tree." So I'm walking, pushing him outside, and my wife at the time is following us, but staying back to be safe. While we're going out the door, this sixty-five-year-old guy who used to work for the company that's having the party, he sees the delirium guy and says, "Hey Theo"... or Leo, whatever the guy's name was... and then the Theo guy socks the old guy right in his head!

So I start pushing Theo the rest of the way out, really fast, but when we get outside, Theo's son-in-law comes out also, and they both attack me! So I drop them both with punches and it's easy—BAM, BAM—and then I smile at my wife and say, "Hey, things are looking good for next week!" (laughs)

Then I hear somebody scream, and I look over and see that Theo is back up and he's running at me again, so I kick him right to the face. But because he's coming at me so fast, I hit him with my shin instead of my foot and... ooooh, that was a bad one, man. Cracked his skull, his teeth were out, his jaw broke... it was really scary.

When the police came to the scene, they looked at his face and then started looking around and asking where I put the baseball bat. They wouldn't believe me that I did that with only my leg! (laughs)

In the hospital, Theo had to get his jaw wired shut. He was in a coma, only half-conscious, and he kept mumbling over and over about razor blades and scissors. When I heard about that, I thought, "Oh no, I kicked him insane"—well, more insane than he already was—and I right away called my brother who is a lawyer. After I told my brother what happened, he said, "You don't remember anything, right? Everything went black, right?" and I said, "...right, yes... everything went black and I don't remember."

After that, the police questioned me, and they kept trying to trick me, asking me what color shirt Theo was wearing and things like that to prove I had a clear mind during the fight. But I just kept saying, "I have no clue, everything went black," and they eventually had to let me go. But because [the damage] was so bad, I had to go to court for this one.

It was an open court, and for some reason a group of women came in to watch, and I had also a female judge. So I went up to the podium where the accused have to stand, and the judge motioned to the women in the audience and said, "Mr. Rutten, it looks like you brought your fan club." And I said, "That's right, let's hear it, ladies!" (laughs) The judge was not happy that I took it to the next level, but I told her, "I'm sorry, but you started it," and she had to smile a little bit at that.

We had the trial, and in the end the judge said, "I don't like it, but because of the evidence I have to let you go." As soon as she said "not guilty," I knew it was over, and now I can say whatever I want. So I look at her and go, "You know exactly what happened and why he got hurt. He hit a guy, then he hit two women including my mother-in-law, then he hit an older guy, and THEN him and his son-in-law attacked me with bad intentions! Trust me, I was in the right." And she gave a little smile again, so I could tell that she was really okay with it.

Thankfully, Theo ended up being okay. Three days after the incident, he woke up and started speaking normal again, thank God. You should understand that [his coma] scared the shit out of me,

(Left to right):
Kenny Rice, me, Bas, and
actor/fighter Chris Bruno
on the set of Kenny and
Bas' long-running series
INSIDE MMA.

I was really scared. The guy had kids, he was even a grandfather. I thought I really messed him up, maybe turned him into a person who's brain dead or something. I didn't sleep for the whole three days he was in a coma, because it really bothered me that he might be permanently injured.

I mean, he deserved it, but I didn't wanna hurt him that bad. Sometimes, going too far is too far.

The Rockefeller

Another club in Holland where I worked was called The Rockefeller—later they changed it to The Bandit—which was in a little village called Schaijk. People from all around, even from the big city, would come to this place because it was an awesome place. It had a really good DJ, his name was Bas also.

The club was at ground level, but they also had these stairs going down under the ground, where there was a little street with a German pub, and an English pub, and a snack bar. So if you were dancing upstairs and you got hungry, you could go downstairs and eat something. It was pretty cool.

Needless to say, troublemakers always "fell from the stairs." If the cops would come to pick up bad people after we beat them up, they would always smile and say, "Fell from the stairs again, Bas?" and I'd say, "Yup! Fell from the stairs." (laughs) That was always our thing because it was a nasty stairs, made of stone, so if they fell from there, they would probably have injuries like the ones we gave them... I think. I guess.

One time, there are these Algerian guys causing trouble, so we have to throw them right away out. Should I say they were Algerians?

I don't want to be racist, I just say it because that's where they were from. Anyway, I throw one of the guys first against the wall, then against the door, then I throw him outside. When that happens, I break the handle on the door with his body—it was made of metal, but I guess it was a different kind of metal, a weaker one, because it broke.

After he is outside, I go to close the door which is a very thick plexiglass that would never break, I think it could even stop a bullet. As I am closing it, the guy looks at me and tells me he is going wait for the right moment and then kill me, and then he slits his throat with his thumb.

Now, those threats you have to take serious. One of my bouncers tells me to come inside, but I say, "No, I'm going to take care of this now," because I don't want to be getting into my car next week, and have him and his friends jump me. I can't take that risk.

So I go outside, and the guy puts up his fists. He was southpaw, right hand forward, and he steps into a REALLY wide karate stance or kung fu stance, I don't know what it was. I think maybe he didn't know either! (laughs) So I right away launch a right-foot round-house kick, full blast in his face, which is even worse for him because I am wearing steel toes. SMASH! It hits him and he goes down on his knees, and his lip is split in half, you can see the lip hanging. And then, because he was going to kill me, I load up for a penalty kick in his face.

This is the part where I am SO lucky here, man.

I kick with everything I have, maximum power, but just as I do that, he falls backwards so I miss, and the force [of the kick] makes me do a complete pirouette. I'm not even finished spinning when I realize that if I connected, he would have for sure died, so as I finish coming around, I put my hands up to the sky and think, "Thank YOOOU!!!" I know I would have kicked a hole in his face and he would guaranteed be dead, and today I would still be in jail and not be in America.

That's one of those moments when you don't think and you go on emotion. I was very, very lucky that I didn't kill this guy.

April 1997: Me and Bas at the Monte Carlo nightclub in Tokyo, Japan.
(I did Duck Face before Duck Face was cool).

Crazy Cocaine Guy

I think the turning point for me when I didn't wanna work at The Rockefeller anymore was when there was a guy outside who was on coke. [He was] known to be a coke addict, like super out of his freakin' mind, and he had a gun that he was pointing at one of my bouncers. So I ran to the kitchen because there we had weapons, and I grabbed a gun, hid it under my shirt, and ran outside. I didn't wanna pull it right away because he was holding the gun in front of my bouncer's face, and he's crazy and he's screaming, you know? I was afraid that if I pull my gun and he sees it, he's gonna shoot my buddy (or at least, the guy who I thought was my buddy).

There's other people around and everybody's freaking out, but finally the guy decides to go away. When he does, I tell the other bouncer not to worry, because I have a gun in case the guy comes back and wants to shoot or something. And the bouncer gets really mad and says, "You had a gun the whole time and you didn't do anything?!!!"

That was the moment where I realized I don't wanna work with these guys. If the situation was reversed and the guy was holding a gun in *my* face—and you should have seen this guy, he was completely out of control like you see on TV—if that happened and the other bouncer pulled a gun, this crazy guy would have pulled the trigger and killed me! When the bouncer blames me for not pulling the gun, I tell him, "Man, if we were in opposite positions and you would have pulled the gun, if I didn't end up dead I would have fucked you up!"

Bas with elite striking coach Carlo Dekkers (right) and the late, great Muay Thai legend Ramon "Diamond"Dekkers. Photo courtesy Bas Rutten.

You can't have that [mentality], that's insecurity. When bouncers start getting insecure, they think a gun can handle anything. When everybody's standing around outside and a guy's swinging a gun, what's he gonna do [if you draw on him]? He's gonna defend himself, and then people are gonna get hurt. That's way too dangerous.

The Pool Cafe

This story happens at a bar that was very close to my home, in a town called Veldhoven. The bar was called Marilyn, but we used to call it The Pool Cafe—I think it is now called Salinas. It was only half a mile away from my house, so sometimes when I am on duty, I don't have to be there. If anything happens, the manager just calls me and I drive over, and now I'm pissed. Since everybody knows me, and knows how fast I can be there, nobody wants to start anything even when I'm gone.

One night when I am in the place, there is a guy who for some reason, I don't know why, tells my wife Karin that he's gonna kick her ass. So Karin comes to me, and she says, "I think you better start stretching, because there's a big, roided guy over there who says that he's gonna kick my ass." I ask, "Why would he say that?" and she says, "I don't know, I never even talked to him before, nothing."

I walk over to where this guy is talking with some chicks, and I say, "Dude, did you just tell my wife you're gonna kick her ass?" He says, "Do you have a problem with that?" (laughs) I go, "She's my WIFE! Of *course* I have a problem with that!" So the guy excuses himself from the ladies, and suddenly he grabs a barstool and lifts it above his head to smash me. But this stupid guy, he doesn't think about how he has no defense when he holds a stool up like that. So stupid, who does that?

He's still got it up there when I clock him with a straight [punch] in the face. The guy goes down to his knees, and then I grab him by the head and I knee his face. The force of the knee makes his head fly back and hit this rail that runs along the edge of the bar, and the rail broke. A big chunk of it, flying through the air. On purpose they didn't fix that rail for a long time after, as a warning to other troublemakers! (laughs) Then I throw the guy outside and I throw his jacket outside, and I don't hear from him any more.

At that time, Karin was going in for driving classes, and the next morning she has a class, but her instructor is late. When he finally shows up, he says, "I'm sorry, it's my idiot son. He's always looking for trouble. Last night, he fought the wrong guy and now his teeth are out and he's messed up." As the teacher describes the fight a bit more, Karin realizes that the guy from last night was the teacher's son! (laughs)

But wait, the story's not over. Now it's a year and a half later. Karin and I are at the same bar and it's New Year's. In Holland, New Year's is like the Fourth of July, everybody has fireworks. So a friend of mine brought a bomb—like, an actual bomb you have to detonate with a battery. So I said, "Oh my God, that's gonna be cool, I wanna do that!" (laughs)

So I load up the bomb, and I go to put it behind a wall so it's not gonna kill anybody, but the electric cable [attached to it] is only fifteen feet. So I think, "There's no way I'm gonna do this." I mean, it's a bomb, we need more wire. Then this other guy comes up to me, he's a little drunk, and he says, "It's okay, Bas, I got it—come with me!" And he opens up the trunk of his car, and starts ripping out speaker cables. I tell him, "Don't do this, you're drunk, and tomorrow you're gonna hate yourself." But he keeps ripping the cables out, saying, "I wanna see the bomb, don't worry about it!"

Bas with professional hockey's all-time best, "The Great One" Wayne Gretzky. Photo courtesy Bas Rutten.

While he's doing this, he looks over and says, "You don't remember me, right?" I say, "No, who are you?" and he goes, "You beat all my teeth out a couple years ago!" I say, "Dude, that was you? You were huge!" and he says, "Yeah, I was on roids, it was roid rage. You did me a favor when you put me in my place. It's cool, no problem."

So we end up detonating the bomb, which is so strong that it blows seven big, thick bricks up out of the ground. It was crazy, it exploded so hard. And then we end up drinking beers together at the end of the night! (laughs)

Funny how it all comes together—first I beat him up, then his father teaches my wife how to drive a car, and then over a year later, he helps me to detonate a fucking bomb! (laughs) It's the wildest thing ever.

Merry Christmas

One year, The Pool Cafe decided to be open on Christmas Day, and Karin and I go there with Leon van Dijk, my training partner who was a pro MMA and Muay Thai fighter, and Leon's girlfriend at the time who was a fighter also. [She was the] European Muay Thai champion and good on the ground also, a real bad-ass chick.

While we are there, this huge guy, like six-five or six-six, he's with his girlfriend and he's hitting the slot machine really hard. A buddy of mine goes over and says something about it, but the guy just does it again. So I go over there and say, "He just told you don't hit the fucking slot machine, what's wrong with you? Come on, man, it's Christmas! You wanna drink a beer or something?" But the guy just says, "Fuck you!" and pushes me. So I look over at Leon and I say, "Mata Leao!"—which of course means, "Lion Killer Choke"—and Leon starts laughing because he knows what's gonna come.

So I push the guy back because I want him to do the same thing back to me, and the fucking stupid-head does it. As he does, I shove his arms to the side and step around behind him, and then I jump up on his back like Rocky when he did that to Thunderlips [in Rocky III]. I put the choke around his neck, and I'm like a koala bear on his back, right? (laughs) And I go really loud, "FIVE... FOUR... THREE..." and by the time I get to "ONE..." boom, he's out. But still I hold it a little bit more, a little bit more... okay, now he's *really* out.

I grab him by the ankles and I start pulling him out [of the bar], when suddenly I get coldcocked in the face, really hard. I look up to see who did it, and it's the guy's girlfriend! But I barely have time to see this when—BAM!—she goes down, totally unconscious. The girlfriend of Leon stepped up and knocked the chick out, one punch! (laughs)

We drag them both out by their feet and leave them outside. After he wakes up, the guy wants to come back in for his jacket because it has the keys from his car, but I say, "No, man, you screwed up. You're not gonna get those keys now." So he walks home, which is good because he's too drunk to drive anyways.

That jacket stayed there for two weeks, and he finally picked it up on a Sunday afternoon when he was sure that I would not be there, and that there would be witnesses around in case I was! (laughs)

Leon's Fries

In Holland, when the bars close at around three o'clock, the snack bars open and you can get all the fried stuff, like french fries and croquettes and things. They are always packed, because everybody's drunk and they wanna eat something greasy.

So one night at 4 AM, me and Leon are inside this fries place. We're the last ones inside before they lock the door, because these places only stay open for one hour. But after a couple of minutes, some other guys are trying to get in, and the owner asks us to tell them that they can't. So we tell them through the front window, but now they're acting like it's our fault! I'm thinking, "Hey, I don't work here!" and I'm pointing at the owner, like, "It's nothing to do with me, don't kill the messenger," you know?

So Leon and I get our food, and the owner unlocks the door so we can go outside. Those guys are still out there, and one of them comes right up to Leon because he's angry that we have food and he doesn't.

Now, while Leon is walking, he has in his left hand a little box with fries, and on the fries is mayonnaise, and he's using his right hand to dip the fries in the mayonnaise and he's eating. So when the angry guy gets close, Leon eats a fry, and then without missing a step—BOF!—he punches the guy in the face! (laughs) Leon hits so hard, man, the guy just drops on the ground. It was so awesome because, just like in a movie, Leon didn't spill ONE FREAKING FRY! (laughs)

So now Leon's walking away, he's smiling from ear to ear and he's eating, the mayonnaise is dripping down, it was hilarious! Just like Bruce Lee with the one-inch punch—BAF! Coolest thing ever.

Simply the BEST. Photo courtesy Bas Rutten.

Lesson In Life

This is funny, you're gonna like this one. It happened around 1990, maybe '91.

I was working in a nightclub where we we didn't wear a uniform, we just wore our normal clothes. At the time, I thought it was cool as shit to wear overalls with a belt, and a black head rag like a biker would wear. Very stupid, but at the time it was cool... I guess. (laughs)

The owner of this club had another club, a famous bar in a big city nearby, and we got a call that there was some guys there causing trouble, and we have to go and help the other bouncers. So everybody's packing [firearms] because we know it's gonna be dangerous, and we go over there.

We're walking in, and I have a gun hidden behind the bib of my freaking stupid suit that I'm wearing. All the people know us, and they're like, "Okay, bad shit is gonna happen now." Suddenly it's very tense, and I think, "Now I have to set the tone."

Everybody stops talking as they look at me, and I'm trying to look cool and in control as I step forward onto the dance floor. But it's dark, and I don't see that there are three steps going down right in front of me. So I take a step into the air and fall HARD to the ground, and my gun slides out and spins all the way to the middle of the dance floor!

Now I'm facedown on the ground and my fuckin' elbow is bleeding, but I keep my poker face as I stand up. Nobody knows what to say or where to look, until finally I say, "It's okay, you guys can laugh." And then they all died laughing! (laughs) I walk over to the gun, and there's no reason to hide it anymore, so I just pick it up and stick it in the front of my belt. Thank God, the guys we were supposed to deal with had already left!

Man, I thought I was so hard, so cool. That shows you that one moment you can be on top of the world, and a split second later you're on your ass. The most hilarious thing ever! (laughs)

@BasRuttenMMA

Facebook.com/BasRutten

www.BasRutten.com

www.O2Trainer.com

www.BodyActionSystem.com

AUTHOR'S BIOGRAPHY

Photo by Karolina Turek.

Paul "The Mauler" Lazenby has over twenty years of experience in the fields of bouncing, close protection, event security, and a variety of athletic pursuits. In 1991, he deadlifted a Canadian record 601 pounds en route to a silver medal at the Canadian Junior Powerlifting Championships. Four years later, he finished third at the Canadian Strongman Championships.

In 1997, after traveling the world as a pro wrestler, Paul flew to Japan to fight in Pancrase Hybrid Wrestling, the top MMA organization in the world at the time, despite a total lack of combat sports experience. In addition to being the first Canadian ever to compete in Pancrase, he also remains the only Canadian to live and train at the original Pancrase Dojo, to fight legendary King of Pancrase Masakatsu Funaki, and to compete in UFC champion Guy Mezger's World Pankration Championships.

Also a sparring partner of UFC/Pancrase champion "El Guapo" Bas Rutten and three-time K-1 USA Grand Prix champion Michael "The Black Sniper" McDonald, Paul retired from competitive fighting in 2005 as the NFC Canadian MMA champion and the undisputed, undefeated Canadian Muay Thai champion—the first heavyweight to hold major Canadian titles in both sports simultaneously.

Now a ring/cageside commentator and MMA journalist/advocate, Paul has called the action for combat sport events in Canada, Jamaica, Costa Rica, Russia, and the USA, while his interviews, articles and essays have been quoted in a wide variety of media including Sam Sheridan's bestselling book *The Fighter's Mind*. Paul was also a founding director of the groundbreaking Mixed Martial Arts Association of British Columbia (MMABC), and he currently serves as a consultant for the immensely popular "Roots of Fight" clothing line/documentary series.

As an actor, stuntman and stunt/fight coordinator, Paul has worked on over 150 film, TV and video game productions. His notable career credits include: the role of Marcus Fenix in the *Gears of War* video game franchise; pro wrestling instructor and onscreen adversary for Vin Diesel; stunt coordinator for the *EA Sports UFC* and *EA Sports MMA* video games; and longtime stunt double for World Wrestling Entertainment Hall-of-Famer Steve Austin.

Paul is also insanely attractive, outrageously charismatic, mind-blowingly intelligent, manly beyond the measurement capabilities of modern technology, and the author of this bio.

🐦 *@MaulerMMA*

🌐 *www.imdb.com/name/nm1342807*

ACKNOWLEDGEMENTS

My sincerest thanks go out to the following. To anyone who belongs on this list but does not find their name here, I am sincerely sorry. All I can say in my defense is that concussions are a BITCH.

Dacosta! of Chocolate Soop for the KICK ASS cover design, and for all the help that he's given my techno-tarded ass over the years.

Dave "Tee Hee" Hoffman for giving a stupid, stubborn, tormented kid a positive direction for energies that would have otherwise been turned toward self-destruction.

Paul Murphy and Paul Sauve for letting me crash on their couch for months, and putting food in a belly that would have otherwise gone empty, well past the point of those things being convenient.

Herman Hocevar for doing those things and too much other stuff to list here. Hepy Birdsday, Herr-mann.

Sudo Kraja and Davey Laughton for... no, I take that back. Fuck those guys.

Akiva "Abbadon" Maas for being the best tag team partner a dude could ask for. And Lenny "Dr. Luther" Olson for making me laugh till I bled out my ears, guiding me through my wrestling career (including the best match of it), and buggin' me into making one of the most important decisions of my life (although I still haven't forgiven you for that flowered singlet, you asshole).

Rob Hayter, Todd "ORS" Scott, Jeff "Quagmire" Osborne, Chris "Fache" Bruno and FILES News Magazine's Robert Yun for being all-around solid and loyal muthafuckas.

Kirk "Flippety" Caouette for being an indescribably unique, generous, talented and inspirational dude.

Lana Battagello for taking it upon herself to keep me as close to sanity as possible during the worst years of my life.

Chris "Mjolnir" Franco for always, always having my back and ensuring that I never lost a fight that really mattered.

"El Guapo" Bas Rutten for being "El Guapo" Bas Rutten. Love you, vato!

Dr. Olga Toleva for being one of the most beautiful people in the whole goddamned world.

Anthony Fulker of the Lazarus Health Project for actually being that better person that most of us say we're trying to be.

Adrian Burke of FUSIONBodybuilding.com for believing in a relative nobody, and supplying me with top-shelf supplements during the many times that I needed but couldn't afford them.

James "Bam Bam" Bamford for going miles out of his way to give me a career in stunts and acting, with nothing in it for himself and for no other reason than that he could. Thank you for changing my life.

Benita Singh for being my favourite brown person in the whole world (except when you're punching me inna head). You rule, Ben!

Jesse Katz of RootsOfFight.com for allowing me to be a part of the coolest combat sport-related venture on the planet.

Diane "Faggle" Constantinescu for failing gloriously on a regular basis and laughing harder than anyone when she does. Also for fixing my broken carcass more times than I could count. Faggle, you're awesome.

My big sister Jilly. A person can be born with family or they can choose their family, and if I hadn't been lucky enough to have you born into mine, I would have chosen you without a second thought.

Vanessa Mills for being tough, freaky and insane in the best ways possible.

Ken Kabatoff for his help with the back cover design, and for his invaluable support overall.

And very, very special thanks to Carlos Leal and Kristel Vines, whose immeasurable selflessness and boundless generosity got the whole ball rolling. Without you guys, there never would have been a Paul "The Mauler" Lazenby. With all the money in the world I could never repay you, and with every word in every language ever invented, I could never completely express my gratitude.

Thanks also to:

Bryan Alvarez, Dr. Robert Armitage, Steve Austin, Don "Natch" Callis, Wallace Chang, Dean Choe, Kellie Cunningham, Justin Currie, Craig Davidson, Gary Dietrich (RIP), Ines Eisses, Wayne Erdman, Ananda Friedman, Mike Fury, Alan "AT Huck" Haugabook, Ariel Helwani, Jay & Monique Janower, The Jeff O'Neil Show, Kirik Jenness, Stevie Juon, Shannon Knapp, Darren Krill, Helen Leong,

Jane Lessard, Dr. Nigel Liang, Angelica Lisk-Hann, LA Hilts, Chris "Heemasex" Logan, Danny Markovitz, Dave Meltzer, Jennifer Mir, "Sweet Daddy" Malcolm Monroe (RIP), Caine "Meat Grinder" Munoz, "Iron Bear" Gary Myers, Arda Ocal, Aleks Paunovic, John Pollock, Kevin Reynolds, Fred Richani, Anthony "One Man Klan" Ruttgaizer (white power), Sam Sheridan, Hebron Shyng, Chael Sonnen, "Mr. Wrestling" Kevin Steen, Dean Thullner, Natasha Trisko, Mark Valley, Ofir Ventura, Princess Wendy, Patrick Wiebe, Pancrase Hybrid Wrestling, and all the people who generously shared their unbelievable stories with me.

COMING SOON

When We Were Bouncers II